PREPARING FOR DISASTER

WHAT EVERY EARLY CHILDHOOD DIRECTOR NEEDS TO KNOW

by Cathy Grace and Elizabeth F. Shores

DEDICATION

To the courageous individuals who lived through Hurricane Katrina with a determination to come back better than before; to the children and families who found comfort and strength in each other and have excelled in spite of trauma; and to those who came and stayed through the bad and the good so that the children of Katrina could laugh again.

and

To Charles Grace of Tupelo, Mississippi, and Buddy Johnson of Little Rock, Arkansas, for sticking with us through wind and high water.

ACKNOWLEDGMENTS

Many individuals and organizations contributed expertise and resources to the Rebuilding After Katrina Initiative. They include all of our colleagues at Mississippi State University, particularly Lynn Bell, Connie Clay, Denise Cox, Lynn Darling, Cathy Hollingshed, JoAnn Kelly, Annjo Lemons, Cheryl Mueller, and Pamela Myrick-Mottley of the MSU Early Childhood Institute and Louise E. Davis of the MSU Extension Service. These friends and advisors also include Gary Asmus, Amy Brandenstein, Carol Burnett, Todd Baptiste, Glenda Bean, Paula Bendel-Smith, Shannon Christian, Nadine Coleman, Jeanne-Aimee DeMarrais, Louisa Dixon, Sr. Donna Gunn, Gail Kelso, Paige Ellison-Smith, Emily Fenichel, Ouida Forsythe, Steven Gross, Sherry Guarisco, George Haddow, Moniquin Huggins, Laura Beth Hebbler, Hal Kaplan, Chad Landgraf, Rev. Bill McAlilly, Mary Ann McCabe, Gail McClure, Wendy McEarchern, Thomas Moore, Festus Simkins, Julia Todd, Joy Osofsky, Linda Raft, Stephen Renfroe, Laurie Todd Smith, Linda Smith, Billy Ray Stokes, Roy Winter, and the entire staff of the Center for Applied Research and Environmental Systems at the University of Missouri, particularly Erin W. Barbaro, Michael Barbaro, Michelle Flenner, and Christopher L. Fulcher. Many other friends of young children also helped rebuild the early childhood sector. We learned from all of them.

GH17992
A Gryphon House Book

PREPARING FOR
DISASTER

WHAT EVERY EARLY CHILDHOOD DIRECTOR
NEEDS TO KNOW

Protect Children During Disasters

Reduce Risks to Children, Staff, and Your Program

Plan for Business Continuity

Communicate with Local Agencies

Conduct Staff Planning Sessions

Learn How to Shelter in Place and Evacuate Children Safely

CATHY GRACE AND ELIZABETH F. SHORES

THE DIRECTOR'S COMPANION TO **AFTER THE CRISIS**

Published by Gryphon House, Inc.
10770 Columbia Pike, Suite 201
Silver Spring, MD 20901
800.638.0928; 301.595.9500; 301.595.0051 (fax)

Visit us on the web at www.gryphonhouse.com

Library of Congress Cataloging-in-Publication Information
Grace, Cathy.
 Preparing for disaster : what every early childhood director needs to know
/ by Cathy Grace and Elizabeth F. Shores.
     p. cm.
Includes bibliographical references.
ISBN 978-0-87659-099-7
1. Early childhood education--Administration. 2. School crisis management. 3. Emergency management. 4. School management and organization. I. Shores, Elizabeth F. II. Title.
LB1139.23.G727 2010
363.11'937221--dc22

                                 2009044838

Bulk purchase
Gryphon House books are available for special premiums and sales promotions as well as for fund-raising use. Special editions or book excerpts also can be created to specification. For details, contact the Director of Marketing at Gryphon House.

Disclaimer
Gryphon House, Inc. and the authors cannot be held responsible for damage, mishap, or injury incurred during the use of or because of activities in this book. Appropriate and reasonable caution and adult supervision of children involved in activities and corresponding to the age and capability of each child involved is recommended at all times. Do not leave children unattended at any time. Observe safety and caution at all times.

CONTENTS

INTRODUCTION

This workbook reflects our experiences in the restoration of the early childhood sector in Mississippi following Hurricane Katrina in 2005. The shock we saw then in the faces and heard in the voices of early childhood program directors in Mississippi then were as close to the effects of war as we hope to witness. We hope this book will simplify the many important and difficult tasks of preparing for disaster so that early care and education providers can rebound from any disaster more easily.

Most early childhood programs in the United States are vulnerable to several kinds of disasters, although the degree of risk varies. Those universal threats include fires; severe storms; epidemics, hazardous material incidents, and other mass casualty incidents; and security threats. Programs may also be vulnerable to threats, including tornadoes, wildfires, hurricanes, earthquakes, and volcanoes that exist only in some geographic areas. Those local threats increase the vulnerability of individual programs, making disaster readiness even more urgent (Mississippi State University Early Childhood Institute, 2007).

The early childhood sector's vulnerability to disasters is a risk factor for young children (Shores, Heath, Barbaro, Barbaro, & Grace, 2008). Without a functioning network of early care and education, parents cannot return to work after a disaster, which prolongs the economic stress on families. Even worse, the loss of familiar child care settings is a profound aftershock for young children who have experienced a disaster firsthand or are witnessing its effects on their families. Without the predictable routine of going to an early childhood program, young children are more likely to suffer traumatic stress disorder. In addition, without a high-quality early childhood program, children with stress disorder are less likely to receive treatment and more likely to experience decades of lingering effects. Therefore, reopening existing early care and education programs after a crisis—at the same or higher levels of quality than before—is critical for the recovery of children, families, and entire communities (Shores, Grace, Barbaro, Flenner, & Barbaro, 2009).

The Rebuilding After Katrina Initiative to repair and re-equip licensed centers in southern Mississippi involved dozens of organizations and funding sources and triggered a new level of interagency collaboration in the state. It was an expensive, exhausting process that took years. Four years after Katrina, there were still few requirements or incentives across the country to prepare young children or the early childhood sector for disasters. We hope this can change. We hope that licensing, rating, and accrediting agencies will implement new standards for disaster readiness that will promote greater resilience for the sector, and thus for young children. However, it will still be the responsibility of individuals to prepare for disasters and reduce the risks.

This book is for the administrator of an early childhood program or family child care home who has decided to be proactive about potential disasters.

The first section describes tasks for the director or other senior administrator(s) to accomplish. The second section describes the responsibilities of staff members, particularly teachers. The third section contains worksheets and other forms that can simplify disaster readiness steps. The last section of the book offers guidelines for staff planning sessions so the staff directors can introduce key responsibilities to teachers and other employees and involve the staff in the ongoing task of disaster readiness. By incorporating all eight planning sessions into the staff meeting schedule each year, you will have a program of continuous professional development on this urgent topic.

The worksheets include the Disaster Readiness Master Plan, a three-page form that allows the director to schedule tasks and set priorities. We recommend that most of the disaster readiness activities be performed annually, but for an early care and education program that has not undertaken disaster readiness before, some tasks will require financial planning and more than a year to complete.

Disaster readiness is a serious responsibility. We commend the directors and staff members of child care centers and family child care homes who undertake the tasks in this workbook and wish you many years of clear skies and rewarding service to young children and their families.

DISASTER PREPAREDNESS:
RESPONSIBILITIES OF THE DIRECTOR

1

As the director or administrator of an early childhood program, you are the best person to handle certain responsibilities of disaster readiness. If you have assistant administrators, you should be able to delegate some of these tasks including the important task of serving as director-designate if you are not able to perform your job during a disaster. These responsibilities fall into five categories:

1. Measures to protect children
2. Measures to reduce risk
3. Measures for business continuity
4. Communication
5. Staff planning sessions

In the rest of this section, we discuss these responsibilities for disaster readiness.

This workbook contains numerous worksheets and forms for individual planning activities (starting on page 75). Be sure to make copies of the worksheets and keep them in a special notebook. Make at least two back-up copies of the notebook, one to give to your substitute director and one to store in another location. The section "Measures for Business Continuity" (see page 15) addresses back-up storage of essential records. The three-page "Disaster Readiness Master Plan" (see pages 76–78) ranks the responsibilities of the director by:

Priority 1: Identify disaster readiness contacts
Priority 2: Review regulatory standards
Priority 3: Perform basic readiness activities
Priority 4: Perform advanced readiness activities
Priority 5: Conduct staff planning sessions

Review this entire workbook before completing your Disaster Readiness Master Plan with target dates for individual activities in the plan. Of course, you may complete the tasks in a different order of priority, if you wish.

TO DO

▶ **Use the Disaster Readiness Master Plan (see pages 76–78) to stay on schedule and follow through with all of the detailed tasks of true disaster readiness.**

MEASURES TO PROTECT CHILDREN

During sudden emergencies or disasters, you or your director-designate must account for your staff, move injured adults away from children if possible, and then help injured staff to protect the children inside your facility, evacuate them to a location outside the facility, or even evacuate them to a location some distance from the facility.

By identifying routes and destinations for sheltering in place or evacuation, you can prepare your staff and the children to move more quickly and safely during a crisis. Also, and this is very important, you will be able to advise families and your local emergency management agency *in advance* about where you plan to shelter or evacuate children.

SHELTERING IN PLACE

In some types of disasters, it is safer to keep the children and staff together inside the facility than to evacuate them to a different location. Select rooms or areas of your facility that are away from windows, doors, and exterior walls. If you are in a flood-risk area, select an additional area on the top floor of your facility. Areas with large flat roofs should be your last choice because flat roofs are particularly vulnerable.

TO DO

▶ **Complete a Shelter-in-Place Diagram (see page 96) for each floor, wing, and building at your facility, showing the route to shelter-in-place locations and including one or more telephone numbers for search and rescue assistance. If your facility is small, your usual classrooms may have to serve as shelters.**
▶ **Use the Shelter-in-Place Checklist on page 95 to furnish each shelter location.**

BUILDING EVACUATION

Some types of emergencies, such as fires, flash floods, or earthquakes, call for evacuating children from the facility. Fire marshals in many states require early childhood programs to designate and mark exits for safe evacuation during fires. Your program can do even more to protect children by designating evacuation destinations where children can be sheltered until it is safe to return to the building or until families arrive.

Select areas outside your facility where you and the staff can gather children and remain out of the way of emergency vehicles. If you are in an earthquake area, choose places that are away from trees or buildings. Otherwise, select areas where children will be sheltered from wind, rain, and sun.

> ▸ **Complete a Building Evacuation Plan (see page 80) for each floor, wing, and building at your facility, showing the route to the evacuation location and including one or more telephone numbers for search and rescue assistance.**

TO DO

OFF-SITE RELOCATION

In an earthquake or other disaster involving localized danger, you may need to evacuate children and staff to a distant or off-site location. If your state and local emergency management agencies have not designated relocation sites for your program, you must find them yourself. If you can designate off-site relocation sites *before* a disaster, you can advise families during the annual orientation, in the family handbook, or by telephone as you evacuate.

Ideally, you should designate off-site relocation sites in two or more directions, in case one route or direction is unsafe. To designate off-site relocation sites, learn your community's general evacuation routes. Study an area map to choose evacuation routes along major roads, avoiding bridges and overpasses where possible. Next, search for specific locations that could shelter your staff and children until they can reunite with families. Perhaps you can establish reciprocal arrangements with early childhood programs in other communities, or ask a church, community center, or school to provide shelter. Identify these off-site relocation locations on the master plan (see page 94).

> ▸ **Use the Emergency Management Liaison Form on page 87 to formally request guidance on community evacuation routes and relocation sites.**
>
> ▸ **Identify relocation sites, either from emergency management agency (EMA) recommendations or through your own research. (Your community should have a municipal or county EMA. This agency is responsible for search and rescue operations after disasters.)**
>
> ▸ **Complete an Off-Site Relocation Plan (see page 94) for each relocation site you designate, copying one or more telephone numbers for search and rescue assistance on the plans. Inside the main box on the form, reproduce a clear map that shows the route and location for the relocation site.**

TO DO

MANDATORY CLOSINGS

You may be ordered to close your facility temporarily because of an approaching hurricane, wildfire, or flood. In a serious epidemic, your public health agency may order early childhood programs and schools to close for a period of time. The health department should have a plan for notifying your program, but it is important to follow news reports about mandatory closings. This is particularly true if you operate a license-exempt program, because the public health agency may not know of your program's existence.

To protect your program's investments and to maintain communication with staff and families during the time the program is closed, you should plan to move computers, key learning materials for each age group, and other hard-to-replace items to a safer location.

You may want to mention explicitly in your parent handbook that the program will continue to collect tuition during a mandatory closing.

TO DO

▶ **Use the Mandatory Closing Checklist on page 93 to plan which items you will move out of the facility and to double-check building security measures before vacating the facility.**

MEASURES TO REDUCE RISK

In the emergency management field, actions that may reduce the damage and losses from disasters are called **mitigation.** As the director or owner of an early childhood program, you may not be able to take the greatest possible mitigation step of moving your entire facility to a safer location. However, you may be able to make structural or non-structural modifications to the facility to reduce the damage if a disaster occurs (Federal Emergency Management Agency, 2006; Institute for Business and Home Safety, 1999; National Association of Child Care Resource and Referral Agencies, 2006; Oregon Natural Hazards Workgroup, 2003).

FACILITY MODIFICATIONS

Many modifications to your facility can reduce the risk of injury or property damage in a fire, explosion, or other disaster. These changes may be expensive, and they may require outside funding. You can hire a qualified contractor to assess your facility's needs for structural modifications and provide an estimate of costs. With this information, you can decide whether the modifications are feasible or whether moving your program to another facility would be wise.

Your insurance carrier may be willing to reduce your premiums if you complete certain modifications. In this case, it could be financially worthwhile to borrow money to make the modifications, knowing you can repay the loan with the savings on insurance premiums. (See the section "Insurance.")

Your local EMA may be able to help you assess your facility or recommend qualified contractors.

▶ **Use the Facility Modifications Needs Assessment on pages 90–92 to assess your facility, to schedule any steps you can take, and to assess any properties your program may need to lease or purchase.**

TO DO

NON-STRUCTURAL MODIFICATIONS

You and your staff can take many steps to reduce the dangers during disasters, such as:

▶ Keeping a NOAA weather radio with tone alert and battery backup in a central location and continually on;

▶ Ensuring that evacuation kits are fully stocked and easily accessible; and

▶ Placing a pipe or crescent wrench next to each water and gas source.

▶ **Use the Child Safety Checklist (on page 82) to assess your facility and schedule the steps that staff members need to take. You can involve your staff in this assessment to make them aware of the importance of the modifications.**

TO DO

MEASURES FOR BUSINESS CONTINUITY

Disasters that cause severe structural damage to your facility or injure many employees could force you to temporarily close your program. An epidemic could lead to mandatory closing of your business for many weeks. Fortunately, you can take the following measures before a disaster to reopen your business as soon as possible.

RECORDS BACK-UP

Back-up storage of business and child records is crucial for business continuity and for supporting children and families in the aftermath of disasters. If your program already uses electronic records, you are a step ahead in disaster readiness. If your program uses paper records, it is wise to plan conversion to electronic records. We recommend that you include conversion to electronic records in the first year of your disaster readiness activities.

Administrative staff members are responsible for maintaining and preserving enrollment records (including emergency contact information) and other business records (including a complete, current copy of your master plan for disaster readiness). Teachers are responsible for the secure storage of child progress records so that in a disaster the records can be recovered. If your program's records are electronic, the specifications of your program's computer system will determine the most efficient means to back up the records, either to a web-based server or on portable disks or hard drives, which can be stored at an administrator's home, a granting agency, or a partner program.

The person responsible for maintaining your computer system should be able to advise you about the most appropriate method of backing up your electronic and paper documents. Several options are available.

TO DO

▸ **Use the Essential Records Back-Up Worksheet on pages 88–89 to complete and implement a plan.**

INVENTORY

If you must file insurance claims after a disaster, you will need a current, accurate inventory of equipment, furnishings, and supplies, by classroom and with purchase price recorded. Complete an inventory of administrative and classroom equipment and furnishings each year.

INSURANCE

Several types of insurance can be important for repairing and reopening your facility after a disaster. Commercial property insurance and homeowner's insurance typically provide some coverage for repairing fire and wind damage. You may need separate policies for flood and earthquake damage (Insurance Information Institute, 2008).

TO DO

▸ **Complete the Disaster Insurance Worksheet on pages 85–86 as a record of the forms of insurance you already have or will purchase for your program.**

RENTAL AGREEMENTS

If your program operates in a rented facility, use the next renewal of the rental agreement as an opportunity to ask the landlord to add specific terms about how quickly he or she will repair damages after a disaster.

DISASTER FUND

Even if your program is fully insured against disasters, having a disaster savings fund will help your business survive because insurance payments may be slow to arrive, or too low to cover all of your program's losses.

An equally important scenario would be a pandemic, where your employees might need to voluntarily stay home from work. Your program could be ordered to close for 12 weeks or longer (U.S. Department of Health and Human Services, 2007). As an administrator, your responsibility is to help protect the health of the general public by complying with the order, even when closing your program will be a hardship for your employees and the families you serve. Providing "underground" child care in private homes will not help stop the spread of disease and could cause more illness and death.

It is a good idea to open a separate bank account for a disaster fund and, over a 12-month period, invest enough to cover all routine operating expenses, including payroll, for at least one month. If your facility is located in an area at risk for two or more kinds of natural disasters, or at risk for disasters not covered by insurance, we suggest that you continue these investments over the next 12-month period so that you create a two-month disaster fund. Continue for a third year so that you eventually have a fund that will cover three months.

To do this, first calculate your annual operating expenses, including payroll, insurance premiums, rent or mortgage payments, all utility payments, transportation costs, and all purchases including food and classroom materials. Divide that amount by 12 to arrive at your goal for your program's one-month disaster fund. Next, divide that amount by 12 again to find the amount you should deposit each month in order to create your disaster fund.

Annual operating expenses ÷ 12 = One-month disaster fund

One-month disaster fund ÷ 12 = Monthly deposit necessary to create the one-month disaster fund within a year.

TO DO

To set aside this money, you will need to reduce your usual expenditures or increase your revenue, or both. A combination strategy may be the easiest to implement. You might decide to find half of the money by reducing discretionary expenditures such as gasoline for field trips and raise the other half through slight increases in tuition.

Whether you decide to reduce expenditures, increase fees, or both, the families in your program will appreciate knowing that you are planning for the long-term security of their children's early childhood program. However, you may need to explain these changes more than once to address families' concerns. Send home a note such as the following to explain the changes:

A LETTER HOME

Be prepared to meet individually with parents and family members who are concerned about the changes in expenditures or fees. In addition, you can prepare an annual "readiness report" to families to explain your program of continuous staff development as well as the amount in the "rainy day fund." Your pride and confidence in preparing your program for disaster will help persuade parents to support your policy.

After calculating how you will pay for your disaster fund, open an account for the fund at a bank with headquarters outside your program's immediate area. This could give your program added protection if a disaster or pandemic affects banks in your local area. (Report the holdings in the disaster account on annual tax returns.)

TO DO

▸ **Complete the Disaster Fund Worksheet on pages 83–84 to plan your program's disaster fund.**

COMMUNICATION

It may be difficult to communicate with employees and with public agencies during a disaster, but effective communication will help your program resume operation sooner.

To stay in touch with your employees during and after a disaster, keep your rosters of employees current and include two or more emergency contacts for each person, so that if employees evacuate the community, you may still be able to reach them.

To simplify communication with public agencies, use copies of the Agency Contact Sheet (see page 79).

▶ Enter contact information for regulatory and funding agencies on your Disaster Readiness Master Plan (see pages 76–78).

▶ Use the Agency Contact Sheet on page 79 to keep track of important communication with agencies. You can duplicate the contact sheet and complete one for each agency or perhaps for each week, or simply use it as a model for notes that you make.

TO DO

EMERGENCY MANAGEMENT AGENCY

Your state EMA may have a good system in place for making sure that local emergency management agencies are aware of all early childhood programs, but it is *your responsibility to make sure* your EMA knows about your program. Your local EMA also may have identified routes and shelters for off-site evacuations and may be able to notify you of these each year. If not, it is *your responsibility to consult your EMA, study road maps, and contact possible shelters* in other communities so that you can advise families in advance where they are likely to find their children after an evacuation.

▶ Use the Emergency Management Liaison Form on page 87 to document your communication with your local EMA. Each year, as you update your program's plan, complete the form and visit your local EMA to deliver the original. Ask for a meeting with an EMA official so you can discuss your facility's location and request guidance on off-site relocation routes. Keep a copy of the completed form in your program's disaster readiness notebook.

TO DO

After a disaster, you should notify the EMA of the following:
▶ Damage to your facility, and
▶ Your program's status (open or closed).

PUBLIC HEALTH AGENCY

In the event of an epidemic or other health-related disaster, your public health agency may order special infection control measures. It may have to order early childhood programs to close temporarily. Your public health agency may have a good system in place for notifying all early childhood programs of steps like these, but it is *your responsibility to find out* what you are expected to do.

It is likely during a disease outbreak that you will need to report to your public health agency the following information:
▶ The number and identities of children enrolled in your program who have become ill as a likely result of the epidemic,

- Your program's compliance with mandatory infection control measures, and
- Your program's compliance with a mandatory closing.

LICENSING AGENCY

If your program is licensed by your state, you should notify your licensing agency contact of your program's status after the disaster. The licensing agency may be the liaison with your public health agency.

After a disaster, you probably will need to provide written reports and/or photographs to your licensing agency of the following:
- Your program's compliance with mandatory infection control measures,
- Your program's compliance with a mandatory closing,
- Damage to your facility, and
- The status of your program (open or closed) pending inspection by the licensing agency.

CHILD CARE SUBSIDY AGENCY

If your program participates in your state's child care subsidy program, the subsidy program will want to know the status of your program after a disaster.

You probably will need to report the following:
- The status of your facility (open or closed),
- Whether your program needs a waiver to allow previously ineligible children to receive subsidies,
- The number of subsidy-participating children who have not appeared during or following the disaster,
- The number of displaced children who need enrollment in your program, and
- Your program's capacity for enrolling displaced children.

CHILD NUTRITION PROGRAM

If your program participates in your state's child nutrition program, that agency will want to know the status of your program after a disaster.

You probably will need to report the following information to your child nutrition program:
- The status of your facility (open or closed),
- The approximate value of food provided by the program that was lost in the disaster,
- Whether eligible children who are quarantined or unable to attend because of a mandatory closing can receive meals by alternate means,
- Whether your program needs a waiver to continue participating in the child nutrition program,
- The number of enrolled children who have not appeared during or following the disaster,
- The number of displaced children who need enrollment in your program, and
- Your program's capacity for enrolling displaced children.

MENTAL HEALTH AGENCY

Your program should have a memorandum of understanding with a mental health agency in order to refer children and families for evaluation and possible treatment.

After a disaster, you probably will need to report the following information to your mental health agency:

▶ Whether the children in your program have experienced trauma,

▶ Your request for in-service training, if available, for teachers and caregivers who are working with children who experienced the disaster, and

▶ Referrals of individual children and families, as necessary.

DEVELOPMENTAL SERVICES AGENCY

Your program should have a memorandum of understanding with a developmental services agency in order to refer children and families for evaluation and possible treatment.

After a disaster, you probably will need to report the following information to the developmental services agency:

▶ Whether the children served by the agency have experienced trauma,

▶ Your request for in-service training, if available, for teachers and caregivers who are working with children who experienced the disaster, and

▶ Referrals of individual children and families, as necessary.

▶ **Establish a memorandum of understanding with a local mental health agency so that your program is ready to make referrals of children and families as needed. To do this, meet with staff members of the agency to find out how they handle referrals from early childhood programs. If they have a standard memorandum of understanding, review it to be sure its terms meet your program's needs. If they do not, simply talk through how you would like to contact them when individual children need assessment. Ask whether they have a standard referral form, or if the state human services department has a standard form. (The referral form should have a section for permission and signature by a parent or guardian.) Ask for a timetable for referrals, that is, the maximum number of days from referral to evaluation and from evaluation to recommendations. Draft a document that specifically explains the responsibilities of your program and the other agency. For example, the agreement could specify that the early childhood program will advise parents of the agency's services and the agency will provide services on a sliding scale of fees.**

TO DO

CHILD CARE RESOURCE AND REFERRAL AGENCY

If there is a child care resource and referral agency (CCR&R) in your community, that agency may be able to give you valuable assistance before, during, and after a disaster.

After a disaster, report the following information to your CCR&R:
- The status of your program (open or closed), and
- Damage to your facility.

STAFF PLANNING SESSIONS

No program is ready for a disaster if the staff has not participated in planning. Staff planning should be ongoing and should offer real opportunities for employees to provide input about how they can best participate during actual disasters.

Plan a series of staff planning sessions each year on topics that are appropriate for staff involvement. You or a facilitator will need to prepare for a planning session on each topic. You may want to plan 2-hour sessions for the first year and have half-day sessions on some topics in alternating years. You may want to have your director-designate or another senior staff member facilitate some of the sessions. The session on first aid probably will need multiple trainers and break-out groups. The next chapter of this book, "Disaster Preparedness: Responsibilities of the Staff" introduces each topic.

TO DO

- **Complete the annual schedule of staff planning sessions in the Disaster Readiness Master Plan (pages 76–78).**
- **Use the Guides for Staff Planning Sessions beginning on page 45 to collect materials and conduct the sessions.**
- **If possible, invite outside speakers to provide more detailed information.**
- **Use the Staff Planning Session Roster on page 99 and Staff Planning Participation Log on page 98 to document your employees' participation in disaster readiness activities.**

You and your staff can have the most positive impact on children's and families' recovery by helping children cope with emotional trauma after experiencing a disaster. Because your potential to reduce chronic stress among children and families is so great, the chapter, "Guides for Staff Planning Sessions," devotes considerable attention to this topic.

DISASTER PREPAREDNESS:
RESPONSIBILITIES OF THE STAFF

2

For most businesses and agencies, administrators can appoint a few employees to serve on disaster preparedness teams and rely on them to spearhead readiness and response activities. However, in early childhood programs, most employees are directly involved in caring for children and cannot be reassigned to full-time disaster preparedness activities, even temporarily. Moreover, employee turnover is high in the early childhood sector, making it important that every new employee become familiar with the program's disaster readiness plan. Ultimately, all employees share the responsibilities of disaster readiness to protect and care for young children.

Through joint planning sessions, you can inform and train your employees about the shared responsibilities of these aspects of disaster readiness:

- Promoting resilience in children
- Implementing child safety precautions
- Practicing infection control
- Understanding basic or advanced first aid
- Assisting with sheltering in place
- Assisting with building evacuations
- Assisting with off-site relocations
- Helping children cope after disasters

The guides for staff planning sessions in this book make up a curriculum for continuous professional development of your early childhood staff on the key responsibilities of disaster preparedness. By sharing responsibility for planning with the staff, and by holding planning sessions on specific topics throughout the year, you can ensure that your staff is genuinely ready to respond if a disaster occurs.

> ▶ **Use the Guides for Staff Planning Sessions (see pages 45–74) to hold a series of training sessions with employees each year.**

TO DO

PROMOTE RESILIENCE IN CHILDREN

Resilience is the capacity to spring back. Emotional resilience is the ability to cope with stressful or traumatic experiences and to recover from them without developing a chronic stress disorder. For this reason, promoting resilience in young children is a very important part of disaster readiness.

Children develop resilience largely from the daily experience of being cared for and protected by adults who respond to their needs and fears and help them practice self-reliance. Through many experiences of tackling small problems and challenges and overcoming them, children can learn to cope with adversity rather than give up.

Teachers and all adults who care for young children are responsible for helping children develop resilience by:

- Providing a primary caregiver for each child,
- Maintaining a predictable daily routine,
- Demonstrating friendship,
- Demonstrating helpfulness and self-reliance,
- Helping children set and meet individual goals,
- Encouraging exuberant play,
- Demonstrating a hopeful outlook, and
- Managing personal stress.

These responsibilities are covered briefly here. Details are in the guide for the staff planning session on promoting resilience on pages 46–53.

PROVIDE A PRIMARY CAREGIVER FOR EACH CHILD

A strong and trusting relationship with a teacher or caregiver helps young children develop the resilience to cope with traumatic experiences (Lieberman & Van Horn, 2004; National Association for the Education of Young Children, n.d.). Frequent changes in caregiver assignments at the child care center or other program can undermine children's sense of security. For children who have had traumatic experiences, teachers should make extra efforts to ensure that the same adults greet those children in the morning, work with them in learning activities, and respond to their needs.

MAINTAIN A PREDICTABLE DAILY ROUTINE

Young children benefit from a predictable daily routine (Grace, 2008). Routines reinforce children's confidence that adults will feed them, sing to them, and help them change their clothes. Routines also help children learn to manage their own emotions. A child who wants to go outside to play can develop patience if he knows that outdoor playtime always follows lunch.

A predictable routine includes regular times for group and individual activities, meals and snacks, indoor and outdoor play and learning activities, toileting, and rest.

DEMONSTRATE FRIENDSHIP

Caring adults can help young children learn how to form friendships and to sympathize with others (Grace, 2008). A friendly child will be better prepared to interact with other children who are in distress, and with strangers in unusual circumstances, such as a disaster.

Teachers and caregivers can do many things to show children how to form friendships:

- When a new child enrolls in the program, ask slightly older children to show him around.
- If a child has important news such as a new baby at home, quietly encourage another child to ask her about her new sister or brother.
- Pay attention to children who are slow to warm up and have trouble joining others at play; model ways to participate:

  Mary, I'm going to ask Janelle and Andrea if I can play with them. Would you like to come with me?

DEMONSTRATE HELPFULNESS AND SELF-RELIANCE

Adults can show young children how to help each other and to help themselves (Grace, 2008). These problem-solving skills enable children to feel more confident during a frightening situation. For example:

  Jason, it looks like Lauryn needs help lifting that bucket. Can you help her?

  Mariah, I can see that's a lot of blocks to carry at one time, but if you make two trips, I think you can do it yourself.

  Luke, would you ask two friends to help you pick up the dishes after snack time?

Preschool-aged and school-aged children can develop self-reliance through problem-solving scenarios. Teachers should make problem-solving scenarios a regular part of the classroom schedule. The following examples (Grace, 2008) can work well with small groups at the Dramatic Play Center or with an entire class during group time.

SCENARIO
Ball in the Street

Describe the problem:

Mary and Marcus were walking along the sidewalk when Mary saw a ball in the street. When she started to get the ball, Marcus said, "Wait Mary! Don't go into the street to get the ball! Don't go!"

Ask the children:

- What might happen to Mary if she goes into the street?
- What is another way that Mary could get the ball?
- Why did Marcus try to stop Mary?

Describe the problem:

Katrina and Marsha were playing with their dolls when Joe came over to see what they were doing. He wanted to play, but the girls told him he could not play. They said, "Leave us alone, Joe!" Joe got mad and hit Marsha with Katrina's doll. Marsha and Katrina both started to cry.

Ask the children:

- What was another way the girls could have talked to Joe?
- What was another way Joe could have shown the girls he was mad?
- Did hitting Marsha help Joe get to play with the girls?
- What was another thing Joe could have done, in order to play with the girls?

Describe the problem:

The sky was cloudy and the wind was blowing. Sheenka and Kendrick were outside playing. They decided to climb a tree.

Ask the children:

- Why do you think they decided to do that?
- What do you think might happen to them?
- What else could they have done?

HELP CHILDREN SET AND MEET INDIVIDUAL GOALS

When a child experiences the success of meeting goals, she develops confidence that will help her face challenges and frightening experiences. She begins to learn that she can break down a problem into smaller parts that she and others can solve.

For example, in helping a small child to dress herself, a teacher can say:

> *"Let's put your right hand through the sleeve. Wonderful!*
> *Now let's put your left hand through the other sleeve. You did it!*
> *Let's pull the sweater into place—hooray! You put on your sweater!"*

Involve children in setting the table for a snack:

> *"Who wants to help me set the table? Johnny, please get the napkins from the basket. Now, put a*
> *napkin at each place.*
> *Shondra, can you put out the spoons? Put one at each place.*
> *Tristan, you can put out the bowls.*
> *Good work, everyone! Together we have set the table."*

Many classroom activities provide opportunities to practice setting goals. For example, children might select three books they want to read; write or dictate a list of the titles; and then check each title off the list after they read it.

ENCOURAGE EXUBERANT PLAY

Daily, physical, exuberant group play can allow children to experience "loving relationships and acceptance, victory and recognition, creative expression, empowerment and control, safety and predictability, joy, humor, and helping others" (Gross, 2007). Play allows children to create and control a world they can master, conquering their fears while practicing adult roles, sometimes in conjunction with other children or adult caregivers. As they master their world, play helps children develop new confidence and the resilience they will need to face future challenges (Ginsburg, 2007).

DEMONSTRATE A HOPEFUL OUTLOOK

In the midst or the aftermath of a traumatic experience, a young child will have trouble finding reasons for hope if she did not already have a hopeful outlook. Adults can demonstrate hope in many large and small ways.

If a child accidentally spills a drink, respond cheerfully:
Well, we can fix that together. Will you help me clean up the spill? Then I will get some more juice for you.

If a child's family is moving away and the child is sad, reassure him:
I know you will miss all of us, but we will write you a letter and you can write back to us.

If a child's parent has lost his job, and the child has overheard his worried parents, say something like:
Your parents must be worried about this, but I know they will find a way to take care of things.

MANAGE PERSONAL STRESS

Caring for young children can be extremely stressful work. The children have many urgent needs; they can be loud; there may not be enough adults for a reasonable adult-child ratio. To make it worse, the salary may be too low for comfort!

Stress management is an important job skill for early childhood professionals not only because the work is stressful but also because the adult's stress level can cause distress in children. A worried, tired, aggravated, or irritable teacher cannot provide young children with the sense of security that is the foundation of emotional resilience.

How can teachers and caregivers manage their own stress in the context of the early childhood program? They can:

▶ Include physical exercise in the daily routine for both children and teachers,

▶ Be honest with the supervisor or director about the challenges of the job, and

▶ Ask for any accommodations that they believe could significantly reduce job-related stress.

IMPLEMENT CHILD SAFETY PRECAUTIONS

Regular drills for fires, tornadoes, and other emergencies are crucial for child safety in an early childhood program, but they are not enough. As discussed in the section "Measures to Reduce Risk" on pages 14–15, there are structural and non-structural modifications to your facility that can make children safer.

Administrators, teachers, and other staff members can help perform annual assessments of safety in the classrooms during the staff planning session "Child Safety Precautions" (see pages 54–55). Employees or teams of employees can inspect all areas of the facility for needed non-structural modifications.

Details are in the guide for the staff planning session on child safety precautions.

PRACTICE INFECTION CONTROL

Young children are at high risk for contracting and spreading communicable diseases. Infection control in early childhood programs is important at all times, especially during seasonal influenza outbreaks and widespread epidemics. You and your staff can help prevent disease outbreaks by getting annual influenza vaccines and encouraging parents and families to have children six months and older vaccinated for influenza as well (Centers for Disease Control and Prevention, 2006).

Your state's health department should have procedures for ordering early childhood programs to close in order to reduce the spread of diseases.

During disease outbreaks, the responsibilities of teachers and other staff members are to:

▶ Practice regular infection control measures,

▶ Remain at home if ill,

▶ Communicate effectively, and

▶ Cooperate with mandatory closings.

The next section addresses each of these responsibilities. Details on this topic are in the guide for the staff planning session on infection control (on pages 56–58).

PRACTICE REGULAR INFECTION CONTROL MEASURES

Your state's licensing requirements probably address hand washing, diaper changing, and other procedures for infection control. Among other steps, staff members should do the following (Dailey, 2004; Centers for Disease Control and Prevention, n.d.):

▶ Stock bathrooms and all sink locations with soap and paper towels or working hand dryers. (If your facility has hand dryers, teach the children the proper way to use them.)

▶ Stock all areas with boxes of tissues and trash cans for used tissues.

▶ Wash hands whenever possible between contact with different children and after touching a child's nose or mouth, helping with toileting or diaper changing or providing first aid or injections.

▶ Wear disposable gloves for any possible contact with blood or bodily fluids such as urine, feces, vomit, or nasal discharge.

▶ Wash hands after removing disposable gloves.

▶ Use soap and water to wash visibly soiled hands.

▶ Use an alcohol-based cleanser when soap is not available or hands are not visibly soiled. **Safety note:** Keep alcohol-based cleansers and all disinfectants out of children's reach.

▶ Help infants and toddlers wash their hands with soap and water before and after eating, and after sneezing and toileting.

▶ Teach toddlers to wash their hands for 15–20 seconds before and after eating, and after sneezing or toileting.

▶ Remind and help children to wash their hands for 15–20 seconds before and after eating, and after sneezing or toileting, even after they have mastered the skill.

▶ Teach toddlers to cover their noses and mouths when sneezing or coughing and to throw away soiled tissues.

▶ Clean frequently used toys and materials daily, using a household disinfectant labeled for bacteria and viruses or a diluted bleach and water solution.

REMAIN AT HOME IF ILL

Employees may be reluctant to miss work even if they become sick. However, voluntary home quarantine is one of the first defenses against epidemics (U.S. Department of Health and Human Services, 2007). Employees need to understand that they may save the lives of the children in the program by remaining at home. If you have established a disaster fund for your program, you may be able to assure the staff that you will continue paying the salaries of absent employees during the disease outbreak.

COMMUNICATE EFFECTIVELY

Staff communication is important during a disease outbreak, particularly if employees or children at the program become sick. Keep your communication strategy simple. As director, you should communicate directly with your second-in-command or director-designate. That person can communicate with a small group such as lead teachers, who can each convey important information to and from the rest of the staff and children's families. Modify this strategy to fit the size of your program.

During a disease outbreak, families and guardians will need regular updates from your program. Prepare a series of daily messages to send home with the children. To prevent miscommunication, the administrator or lead staff member should determine the daily message for families. Teachers or assistant teachers can pass this message on to families of children in their classes.

COOPERATE WITH MANDATORY CLOSING

Social distancing is the practice of voluntarily avoiding public spaces and large groups during epidemics to reduce contact between sick and uninfected persons. It is an important strategy for communities that are in the midst of disease outbreaks (U.S. Department of Health and Human Services, 2007).

In severe epidemics, public health agencies may order schools and early childhood programs to close, which may lead to a high demand for unauthorized child care because parents will still need to get to their jobs. You and your employees probably will feel concern and compassion for these parents and family members who are desperate for alternative child care arrangements, but to help end the outbreak, you and your staff must refrain from offering "underground" child care in your homes or other facilities.

TO DO

▸ **Use the Disaster Fund Worksheet on pages 83–84 to start a savings account so that you can continue to pay employees' salaries while they remain at home because of a disease outbreak or a mandatory closing.**

UNDERSTAND BASIC OR ADVANCED FIRST AID

All staff members should receive annual training in basic first aid, including how to use the contents of a basic first aid kit. Some staff members should receive annual training in advanced first aid for these situations (Mayo Clinic, 2008):

Bites (animal, insect, snake, spider)	Head injuries and concussions
Broken bones	Heat illness
Burns	Severe bleeding
Chemical burns	Shock
Chemical splash in the eye	Storing human remains
Cuts	Sudden cardiac arrest
Dehydration	Tooth loss
Electrical shock	Transporting injury victims
Eye injuries	Vomiting
Falls	

Your state's licensing requirements may stipulate what kind of basic first aid training your staff must receive. Local chapters of the American Red Cross usually offer first aid and cardiopulmonary resuscitation (CPR) classes. Find out if American Red Cross trainers can deliver training at your facility and schedule a staff planning session with them. You may be able to organize your staff planning session on this topic as an all-day workshop with morning and afternoon sessions on basic first aid and breakout sessions for individual employees and teams of employees to receive training on advanced first aid techniques.

Next, you may need to contact your local hospital or area health education center to find more trainers for specialized first aid topics. Child care resource and referral agencies and professional associations also may have lists of qualified trainers on first aid topics. Allow yourself plenty of time for locating and scheduling all of the outside trainers you will need, or delegate the scheduling to an assistant administrator.

SHELTER IN PLACE

Some states require early childhood programs to conduct tornado drills as well as fire drills, because tornadoes require centers to shelter in place by protecting the children in the safest areas inside buildings.

Sheltering in place also may be necessary during security threats, wildfires, severe storms, hazardous material and mass casualty incidents, flash floods, and volcanic eruptions.

In most of these situations, firefighters, police officers, military troops or other first responders will be responsible for rescuing children and staff members. However, staff members must:

- Know designated shelter-in-place locations,
- Escort children,
- Help children cope,
- Participate in safety measures,
- Communicate effectively, and
- Care for children.

In this section, we will briefly discuss each of these responsibilities. Details on this topic are in the guide for the staff planning session on sheltering in place (see pages 61–63).

KNOW DESIGNATED SHELTER-IN-PLACE LOCATIONS

Employees can use the Shelter-in-Place Diagram and the Shelter-in-Place Checklist (see pages 96 and 95) to locate and assess each shelter location. This will give them hands-on knowledge of the locations and procedures for sheltering in place and will help you maintain fully equipped shelters.

TO DO

- **Post a Shelter-in-Place Diagram (see page 96) in each classroom and area of your facility and review routes to shelter locations during your staff planning session.**

Employees must know the designated room or area for storing bodies of anyone who suffers fatal injuries during the disaster.

ESCORT CHILDREN

The Building Evacuation Diagram includes these safety measures for safely escorting children:

- Gather child records and identification tags,
- Place the tags on the children (see the following page),
- Check each room to make sure no child is left behind, and
- Mark the door of each room with an "X" to indicate all children have been evacuated.

> **Ask teachers to create sets of Child Identity Tags (see page 81) for children in their rooms.** These tags can be completed by hand on paper and inserted into plastic holders with clips attached.

HELP CHILDREN COPE

As discussed in the section "Promote Resilience in Children" on pages 24–28, infants and young children have a fundamental developmental need to believe that the adults in their lives will protect them and respond to their needs.

While an emergency or disaster is happening, staff members can reduce children's risk of stress disorder by shielding them from frightening scenes, maintaining a calm air, and repeatedly assuring them that they will be safe. Helping children remain calm will make it easier to protect them and deal with the immediate problems of the disaster.

> **Post the Shelter-in-Place Procedures (see page 97) in each shelter location to help staff members. Written procedures will help staff members remain calm.**

Schedule the staff planning session "Helping Children Cope After Disasters."

PARTICIPATE IN SAFETY MEASURES

Seal the Shelter: If you must shelter the children at your program because of airborne hazardous materials, you and your staff will need to seal the shelter-in-place locations from outside air.

> **Post the Shelter-in-Place Procedures (see page 97) in each designated shelter-in-place location to help the staff remember the steps for sealing a room.**

Rescue Children: In an earthquake, flash flood, explosion, or other disaster that damages the building without warning, staff members may have to assist in rescuing and transporting injured children from debris. If possible, employees with advanced first aid training should direct rescues.

COMMUNICATE EFFECTIVELY

Staff communication is important in a shelter-in-place situation. Keep your communication strategy simple. As director, you should communicate directly with your second-in-command or director-designate. That person can communicate with a small group such as lead teachers, who can each convey important information to and from the rest of the staff and parents. You can modify this strategy to adapt to a larger or smaller staff.

If children and staff members are sheltered in more than one area of your facility, staff should communicate by cell phones, if possible, to report the status of their groups to the lead staff member involved in the emergency.

The lead staff member should call 911 or the local emergency management agency to request assistance or rescue.

Parents and guardians must be informed of their children's status as soon as possible. To prevent miscommunication, the lead staff member should determine the message for parents as soon as possible after gathering the children in shelter-in-place locations.

CARE FOR CHILDREN

Staff members should continue to care for the children until rescuers arrive or, in the case of tornadoes, the National Weather Service announces that the threat has passed. Instructions in the Shelter-in-Place Procedures (see page 97) should help staff members remember to:

- Keep children away from doors, windows, and exterior walls.
- Help children take cover under sturdy furniture or braced against inside walls (if falling debris is a risk).
- Show children how to crouch down and protect their heads and necks with their arms (if falling debris is a risk).
- Monitor a National Oceanic and Atmospheric Administration (NOAA) weather radio for warnings.
- Reassure the children that they are as safe as possible.

ASSIST WITH BUILDING EVACUATIONS

Most early childhood professionals have practiced fire drills and know how to safely and quickly move children out of a building and a safe distance away. Your state's child care licensing requirements stipulate how often you should have fire drills. Earthquakes, interior security threats, and hazardous material incidents also call for sudden building evacuations. If your program has more than 10 employees, you probably have a written evacuation plan to meet requirements of the federal Occupational Safety and Health Administration (OSHA). However, these procedures and requirements may not fully cover the responsibilities of an early childhood program.

The key responsibilities of staff members during building evacuations are to:
▸ Know designated evacuation locations,
▸ Escort children,
▸ Help children cope, and
▸ Communicate effectively.

In this section, we will briefly discuss each of these responsibilities. Details on this topic are in the materials for the staff planning session on building evacuations (see pages 64–66).

KNOW DESIGNATED EVACUATION LOCATIONS

Evacuation locations may be different in different emergencies or disasters. During fires and interior security threats, moving children to the nearest safe indoor location is appropriate. In earthquakes, however, employees should keep the children together in an open area away from buildings, trees, streetlights, and utility wires.

ESCORT CHILDREN

The Building Evacuation Plan (see page 80) includes these safety measures for escorting children safely:
▸ Gather child records and identification tags,
▸ Lead children to safe areas outside, using the same procedures as for field trips,
▸ Check each room to make sure no child is left behind,
▸ Mark each room's door with an "X" to indicate all children have been evacuated, and
▸ Tag children as soon as they are safely outside the building.

HELP CHILDREN COPE

As we discussed in the section "Promote Resilience in Children," the belief that the adults in their lives will protect them and respond to their needs is a fundamental developmental need for infants and young children.

While an emergency or disaster is happening, staff members can reduce children's risk of stress disorder by shielding them from frightening scenes, maintaining a calm air, and repeatedly assuring them that they will be safe. Helping children remain calm will make it easier to protect them and deal with the immediate problems of the disaster.

TO DO

▶ **Schedule the staff planning session "Helping Children Cope After Disasters."**

COMMUNICATE EFFECTIVELY

If children and staff members gather at more than one evacuation location, staff should communicate by cell phones, if possible, to report the status of their groups to the lead staff member involved in the emergency.

The lead staff member should call 911 or the local emergency management agency to request assistance or rescue.

As director, you should communicate directly with your second-in-command or director-designate. That person can communicate with a small group such as lead teachers, who can each convey important information to and from the rest of the staff and parents. You can modify this strategy for a larger or smaller staff.

Parents and guardians will need to know where their children are as soon as possible. To prevent miscommunication, you, your director-designate, or the lead staff member should determine the message for parents as soon as possible after evacuating the children.

ASSIST WITH OFF-SITE RELOCATIONS

Most early childhood professionals have practiced fire drills and know how to safely and quickly move children out of a building and a safe distance away. Your state's child care licensing requirements stipulate how often you should have fire drills. Earthquakes, interior security threats, and hazardous material incidents also call for sudden building evacuations. If your program has more than 10 employees, you probably have a written evacuation plan to meet requirements of the federal Occupational Safety and Health Administration (OSHA). However, these procedures and requirements may not fully cover the responsibilities of an early childhood program.

The key responsibilities of staff members during off-site evacuations are to:
) Know off-site relocation plan,
) Escort children,
) Help children cope, and
) Communicate effectively.

In this section, we will briefly discuss each of these responsibilities. Details on this topic are in the guide for the staff planning session on off-site relocation (see pages 67–69).

PREPARE EVACUATION KITS

A copy of the facility's Off-Site Relocation Plan (see page 94), or copies of multiple plans if you have designated more than one possible relocation site, should be stored in every evacuation kit. Every program vehicle should have a kit and one should be stored near every exit. The kits should contain:
) First aid supplies,
) Goggles for all children and adults,
) Disposable breathing masks for all children and adults,
) Child Identity Tags,
) Child and employee rosters,
) Current Off-Site Relocation Plans, and
) Current state highway map.

As teachers and other employees assist in escorting children to vehicles, they should carry the kits with them. See the Child Safety Checklist on page 82 for more information.

In addition, you should update your program's relocation plans annually, in consultation with the local emergency management agency, and review the plans and relocation sites with the staff in annual staff planning sessions.

ESCORT CHILDREN

The Off-Site Relocation Plan includes these safety measures for safely escorting children:
) Assign adults to assist non-ambulatory children,
) Gather children as quickly as possible; use the buddy system,

- Gather essential prescription medications,
- Remain calm so you can calm the children,
- Carry cell phones,
- Carry battery-powered NOAA weather radio(s) to monitor reports of safe travel routes,
- Do not use elevators,
- Escort children to vehicles, using the same procedures as for a field trip,
- Once children are secure, call 911 or the local emergency management agency to request rescue, and
- Pin Child Identity Tags (see page 81) to children as soon as they are safely in vehicles.

HELP CHILDREN COPE

As we reviewed in the section "Promote Resilience in Children," the belief that the adults in their lives will protect them and respond to their needs is a fundamental developmental need for infants and young children.

While an emergency or disaster is happening, staff members can reduce children's risk of stress disorder by shielding them from frightening scenes, maintaining a calm air, and repeatedly assuring them that they will be safe. Helping children remain calm will make it easier to protect them and deal with the immediate problems of the disaster.

Schedule the staff planning session "Helping Children Cope After Disasters" (see pages 70–74).

COMMUNICATE EFFECTIVELY

If children and staff members gather at more than one relocation site, employees should communicate by cell phones, if possible, to report the status of their groups to the lead staff member involved in the emergency.

The lead staff member should call 911 or the local emergency management agency to request assistance or rescue.

As director, you should communicate directly with your second-in-command or director-designate. That person can communicate with a small group such as lead teachers, who can each convey important information to and from the rest of the staff and the children's parents and guardians. You can modify this strategy for a larger or smaller staff.

Parents and guardians will need to know where their children are as soon as possible. To prevent miscommunication, you, your director-designate, or the lead staff member should determine the message for parents and guardians as soon as possible after evacuating the children.

HELP CHILDREN COPE AFTER DISASTERS

Individual children will react to disasters differently. Some young children will have temporary reactions to traumatic experiences but will recover without clinical diagnosis and treatment if parents, teachers, and caregivers provide secure environments and outlets for expressing fears. Other young children can develop stress disorders after experiencing disasters or other traumas (Alat, 2002; Scheeringa, 2008). Although these disorders are known as Acute Stress Disorder (ASD) and Post-Traumatic Stress Disorder (PTSD), Greenspan & Wieder (2006) suggest that a single term, Traumatic Stress Disorder, is more appropriate for infants and young children who "often respond to severe trauma or stress immediately" (p. 153). Young children who experience disasters actually may experience more severe stress disorders than older children or adults (Drell, Siegel, & Gaensbauer, 1993; McGinn & Spindel, 2007; Somasundaram & van de Put, 2006).

Stress disorders require diagnosis and treatment by mental health professionals, but staff members, and particularly teachers, also have responsibilities for helping children cope in the aftermath of disasters. Those responsibilities are to:

- Manage their own stress,
- Provide a safe environment for children,
- Provide outlets for children's expression,
- Observe and record signs of stress disorders in children, and
- Participate in referrals to mental health professionals.

In this section, we will briefly discuss each of these responsibilities. Details on this topic are in the guide for the staff planning session on helping children cope after disasters (on pages 70–74).

MANAGE STRESS

Teachers are not immune from stress. If teachers experienced the disaster personally or are exposed to the disaster's aftermath, they may feel overwhelmed, anxious, and unable to cope (Osofsky, 2004a). The children's anxiety may increase their own anxiety. Equally important, teachers' anxiety may add to the children's stress. For the children's sake, staff members must maintain a calm, confident air around the children so they will feel protected and safe (Alat, 2002).

As an administrator, you should pay close attention to whether your employees' stress is affecting their work. Encourage employees to be honest about how much stress they feel. At the first signs of problems, you should talk with your employees or their supervisors. Provide help in the classrooms. Bring in an outside stress management counselor and help your employees find help from health care providers or crisis counselors. If your community has experienced a large-scale disaster, there should be extra counseling available for individuals in the helping professions, including teachers. Osofsky (2004) suggests that therapists who work with young children who have experienced trauma should not work in isolation; this is good advice for teachers and caregivers, too. If teachers in your program do not have full-time classroom assistants, encourage them to touch base with each other as often as necessary for advice and support.

PROVIDE A SAFE ENVIRONMENT FOR CHILDREN

The most important developmental need of young children is security—the confidence that the adults in their lives will protect them and relieve their fears and anxieties (Lieberman & Van Horn, 2004). Teachers have a profound responsibility to support children's sense of safety. This becomes even more important after a disaster (Devall & Cahill, 1995).

To provide a safe environment for young children who have experienced a disaster:

- **Give physical comfort:** Hold, stroke, rock, and gently speak to infants and children who are frightened. For children old enough to understand, explain the ways your program keeps them safe (Drell, Siegel, & Gaensbauer, 1993; National Child Traumatic Stress Network, 2008b). Shield children from television and radio reports and adult conversations about the disaster they experienced.

- **Listen and respond:** Attend to children's expressions of fear and anxiety and their retelling of their stories of the disaster (Alat, 2002; Gaensbauer, 2004). Respond with statements like:

  I understand that remembering the flood is scary for you. Do you want to talk more about it right now?

  I can tell you miss your brother very much. Could we draw a picture of him or look at some pictures of him?

  When children describe their experiences in the disaster or ask questions about the disaster, help them handle fear and anxiety by responding simply and honestly:

  Our wildfire happened because the trees were dry and it was very windy. When wildfires happen, the firefighters let people know if they need to go somewhere else to be safe.

  Yes, the storm was very scary for all of us. I'm glad it's over now.

  I was worried that my house was gone. The roof, which is the top of the house, did blow away but the walls were still there.

  I am so sorry that your grandmother died. I know you must miss her very much. Does it help to think about happy times you had with her?

- **Restore or create a familiar, predictable classroom routine:** Knowing what comes next in the day gives children a feeling of control over their lives. Maintain a predictable schedule; reread favorite books; replay favorite games (Osofsky, 2004).

- **Give extra attention to children's needs during transitions:** Group activities and classroom transitions can be challenging for all children, and especially children who have experienced trauma (Lieberman & Van Horn, 2004). Give children a five-minute warning before asking them to change activities and allow them extra time to move from one activity to another. Lead the children in a clean-up song, rhyme or activity to make the transition more fun and productive. Ask children who have the most trouble with transitions to serve as helpers to the teacher and give them specific jobs to perform.

- **Provide quiet areas:** Children who have experienced disasters may seek respite from noise and activity (Demaree, 1995). Make sure your classroom quiet areas have clear sight lines to the places where you sit and stand, so children can be sure that you are nearby.

- **Provide times for outdoor play:** Running, climbing, and organized games may help children channel aggressive emotions.

- **Avoid punitive time-outs:** Forced time-outs can be too frightening for children who have experienced disasters (Demaree, 1995). Children who are experiencing separation anxiety as a result of trauma may cling to adults. When children are unable to participate in class activities because of possible traumatic stress disorder, a caring adult should comfort them, acknowledge their fears, talk in simple terms about how the frightening experiences will not recur in the classroom, and redirect them to positive activities. Children with severe behavior problems may need referral to early childhood mental health specialists.

PROVIDE OUTLETS FOR CHILDREN'S EXPRESSION

Early childhood teachers do not have the background or skills to provide therapy to children with traumatic stress disorder. However, they can do a great deal to help young children cope with disaster experiences. Within the familiar setting of the classroom, they can offer children many opportunities to discuss, reenact, and begin to understand their experiences and feelings—opportunities that can help children deal with stress (Greenspan & Wieder, 2006).

By reading appropriate children's books as the starting point, during group time or with small groups of children, teachers can create many opportunities for creative expression through dramatic play using toy rescue vehicles, dolls, and other props and through writing and art activities and extended projects (Devall & Cahill, 1995; Alat, 2002; Szente, Hoot, & Taylor, 2006). The teacher's goal is not to use the children's traumatic experiences as springboards for meeting curricular objectives in literacy, mathematics, or science, but to support children's deep emotional need to regain a sense of security.

When teachers give children creative outlets for remembering traumatic experiences and expressing fear, anger, and other emotions, they can expect children to describe or depict disturbing events and demonstrate strong feelings. Remembering and reenacting the disaster is appropriate and not necessarily a sign of problems. Teachers are not the right professionals to interpret children's writing samples and artworks as evidence of mental health problems. If teachers share children's stories or artworks related to their disaster experiences with parents and guardians or mental health professionals, they should make clear whether they elicited the storytelling and depiction. Otherwise, the children's work samples could be misinterpreted (Kindler, 1996).

Our companion book for teachers, *After the Crisis: Using Storybooks to Help Children Cope*, contains recommendations for using 50 children's books to help children cope after a disaster. As teachers experiment with these books and activities with the children in their classrooms, they will find that some are more effective than others. We encourage teachers to return to the children's favorite books to repeat or extend activities. You may want to purchase copies of the books that resonate most powerfully with the children in your program.

OBSERVE, RECORD, AND REPORT SIGNS OF STRESS DISORDERS IN CHILDREN

We cannot over-emphasize the fact that teachers are not qualified to evaluate children for medical conditions such as Acute Stress Disorder (ASD) and Post-Traumatic Stress Disorder (PTSD). However, they are the appropriate helping professionals to observe children in the classroom and make written records of incidents or behavior of concern. Teachers should report such signs to a supervisor, to you, and to the children's parents and guardians.

The signs of possible stress disorders are fairly easy to see in children's behavior. Acute Stress Disorder (ASD) occurs from two days to four weeks following the traumatic experience. Post-Traumatic Stress Disorder (PTSD) is a longer-lasting condition and can be diagnosed in children and adults when the symptoms of ASD, or other symptoms, appear to last more than four weeks. Children with ASD or PTSD may:

- Demonstrate separation anxiety or clinginess,
- Complain of physical ailments that may be minor or imaginary,
- Regress in previously mastered skills such as baby-talk or toileting mishaps,
- Develop new skills and concepts more slowly than before the disaster,
- Appear withdrawn or emotionally numb,
- Eat considerably more or less than before the disaster,
- Act angry or uncooperative,
- Seem to have an unusual startle reflex in reaction to bright lights, sudden movements, or loud sounds,
- Express fears about the disaster or about safety,
- Express new fears such as fear of the monsters or the dark,
- Have new or greater difficulty with routine or unexpected transitions,
- Have difficulty remembering details of the traumatic event,
- Seem to feel detached from their bodies or to be in a dream-like state,
- Repeatedly reenact disaster experiences during dramatic play or depict them in artwork, or
- Avoid reminders of the traumatic experience.

(Drell, Siegel, & Gaensbauer, 1993; McGinn & Spindel, 2007; National Child Traumatic Stress Network, 2008a)

If your staff does not already practice anecdotal recordkeeping, it is important to begin to implement this form of assessment during or following a disaster (Shores & Grace, 1998). Later, you may want to work with teachers to expand this practice to areas of the curriculum such as literacy development.

PARTICIPATE IN REFERRALS TO MENTAL HEALTH PROFESSIONALS

Ideally, your early childhood program has a working relationship with a mental health care agency that can evaluate and treat children with possible stress disorders. The teacher should be prepared to discuss his opinion that a child needs evaluation with the child's parents or guardians and with mental health professionals.

It is important to reassure parents at the same time that you make them aware of your professional concern. Explain that stress disorders are common among young children who experience disasters or other traumatic events. Qualified health care workers can help their children recover from ASD and PTSD.

GUIDES FOR STAFF PLANNING SESSIONS

3

PROMOTING RESILIENCE IN CHILDREN

Page 1 of 8

Before the Planning Session

☐ Review the relevant material in the section Responsibilities of the Staff (pages 23–28) and prepare to discuss.

☐ Schedule one or more staff planning periods, depending on the size of your program's staff.

☐ Collect one or more small bouncy rubber balls and one or more partially deflated rubber balls.

☐ Create a comment box from a shoebox or other carton with a lift-off lid. Cut a slit in the lid. Label the box "Stress Box."

☐ Make copies of the reproducible Stress Slips (see page 49).

☐ Make copies of the handout Sample Daily Schedule (see page 50).

☐ Make copies of the handout Problem-Solving Scenarios for Young Children (see pages 51–53).

☐ Make a copy of the Staff Planning Session Roster (see page 99) (make copies if necessary).

☐ Review the next section and decide whether to complete the session in 2 hours or allot more time.

During the Planning Session

☐ Review the Goal and Objectives of the session:

Goal | ▸ To strengthen children's emotional resilience so they can cope with traumatic experiences

Objectives | ▸ To understand the concept of resilience
▸ To practice classroom activities and interactions that promote resilience

☐ To introduce the concept of resilience, bounce a bouncy ball to a staff member and ask her to "bounce it on" to another staff member. If you have another ball, bounce it to another employee. Once the bouncing is underway, toss the semi-deflated ball to a third employee and ask the group to watch him "bounce it on."

☐ Comment that the semi-deflated ball is not resilient, and then define emotional resilience:

Emotional resilience: The ability to recover from or adjust to misfortune or change; the capacity to "bounce back."

PROMOTING RESILIENCE IN CHILDREN

Page 2 of 8

☐ Invite discussion.

☐ Introduce the key responsibilities of the staff for promoting resilience in children:

- ▸ Provide a primary caregiver for each child
- ▸ Maintain a predictable daily routine
- ▸ Demonstrate friendship
- ▸ Demonstrate helpfulness and self-reliance
- ▸ Help children set and meet goals
- ▸ Encourage exuberant play
- ▸ Demonstrate a hopeful outlook
- ▸ Manage personal stress

☐ Discuss the importance of having a primary caregiver for children to feel safe and secure. Ask teachers to discuss how they designate a primary caregiver for each child.

☐ Distribute and review the handout Sample Daily Schedule. Discuss the value of a predictable routine. Ask teachers to implement schedules in their classrooms if they have not done so.

☐ Discuss the value of friendship skills. Ask the staff to discuss situations in which children have trouble forming and maintaining friendships. Brainstorm methods to help the children.

☐ Discuss the value of problem-solving skills as the foundation for self-reliance. Distribute and review the handout Problem-Solving Scenarios for Young Children. Ask teachers to brainstorm ways to incorporate similar conversations into classroom life.

☐ Ask teachers: "Have you experienced the satisfaction and confidence that comes from meeting a goal?" Allow a short time for discussion. Ask: "Do you think the children in our program have enough opportunities to set and work toward their own goals? How can we give them more opportunities to do this?"

☐ Discuss the value of exuberant play. Look again at the Sample Daily Schedule and discuss times in the day when teachers can plan games and gross motor activities. Ask the staff members to brainstorm examples of exuberant play in the following categories:

- ▸ Adult-directed
- ▸ Child-initiated
- ▸ Indoor
- ▸ Outdoor

PROMOTING RESILIENCE IN CHILDREN

Page 3 of 8

☐ Discuss the value of a hopeful outlook. Allow a short time for discussion.

☐ Discuss the importance of personal stress management. Share an example of a time when stress in your own life made it difficult for you to give children the emotional security they needed. Ask staff members: "Can anyone share another example of how stress in our lives can affect the children?"

Encourage the staff to:

> ‣ Include physical exercise in the daily routine for both children and teachers,
> ‣ Be honest with the supervisor or director about the challenges of the job, and
> ‣ Use stress slips to ask for accommodations that could significantly reduce job-related stress.

Distribute Stress Slips and invite the staff to complete them and deposit them in the Stress Box. Promise to respond to the Stress Slips.

☐ Have all participants complete the Staff Planning Session Roster.

After the Planning Session

☐ Follow up with staff on all questions and comments that you recorded.

☐ Acknowledge Stress Slips: Follow up with individual staff members or in the next general staff meeting. Be sure to respect the confidentiality of all staff.

STRESS SLIPS

Page 4 of 8

Duplicate this page and cut the Stress Slips apart. Keep a stack beside the Stress Box.

STRESS SLIP

Share your stress with your supervisor:

_____

_____

_____

_____

_____

Optional:

☐ I would like to meet to discuss this issue.

_____
Signature

STRESS SLIP

Share your stress with your supervisor:

_____

_____

_____

_____

_____

Optional:

☐ I would like to meet to discuss this issue.

_____
Signature

SAMPLE DAILY SCHEDULE

Page 5 of 8

Use this blank schedule to plan a predictable routine for the children in your care. (Omit whole-group activities for infants and toddlers.)

TIME	PREDICTABLE ACTIVITY
☐☐:☐☐ to ☐☐:☐☐	Arrival and Book Time
☐☐:☐☐ to ☐☐:☐☐	Morning Circle or Group Time
☐☐:☐☐ to ☐☐:☐☐	Morning Snack
☐☐:☐☐ to ☐☐:☐☐	Learning Centers Time
☐☐:☐☐ to ☐☐:☐☐	Playground Time
☐☐:☐☐ to ☐☐:☐☐	Hand Washing and Restroom Break
☐☐:☐☐ to ☐☐:☐☐	Lunch
☐☐:☐☐ to ☐☐:☐☐	Hand Washing and Restroom Break
☐☐:☐☐ to ☐☐:☐☐	Rest Time
☐☐:☐☐ to ☐☐:☐☐	Hand Washing and Restroom Break
☐☐:☐☐ to ☐☐:☐☐	Afternoon Snack
☐☐:☐☐ to ☐☐:☐☐	Playground Time
☐☐:☐☐ to ☐☐:☐☐	Learning Centers Time
☐☐:☐☐ to ☐☐:☐☐	Afternoon Circle Time
☐☐:☐☐ to ☐☐:☐☐	Departure

PROBLEM-SOLVING SCENARIOS FOR YOUNG CHILDREN

Page 6 of 8

SAMPLE PROBLEM-SOLVING SCENARIOS FOR FOUR-YEAR-OLD CHILDREN

Incorporate brief conversations like these with children during circle time, group time, and snack or meal times.

Ball in the Street

Describe the problem:

Mary and Marcus were walking down the sidewalk when Mary saw a ball in the street. When she started to get the ball, Marcus said, "Wait Mary! Don't go into the street to get the ball! Don't go!"

Ask the children:

▸ What might happen to Mary if she goes into the street?
▸ Why did Marcus try to stop Mary?
▸ What is another way that Mary could get the ball?

Joe Gets Mad

Describe the problem:

Katrina and Marsha were playing with their dolls when Joe came over to see what they were doing. He wanted to play, but the girls told him he could not play. They said, "Leave us alone, Joe!" Joe got mad and hit Marsha with Katrina's doll. Marsha and Katrina both started to cry.

Ask the children:

▸ What was another way the girls could have talked to Joe?
▸ What was another way Joe could have shown the girls he was mad?
▸ Did hitting Marsha help Joe get to play with the girls?
▸ What was another thing Joe could have done in order to play with the girls?

Climbing a Tree

Describe the problem:

The sky was cloudy and the wind was blowing. Sheenka and Kendrick were outside playing. They decided to climb a tree.

Ask the children:

▸ Why do you think they decided to do that?
▸ What do you think might happen to them?
▸ What is something else they could have done?

PROBLEM-SOLVING SCENARIOS FOR YOUNG CHILDREN

Page 7 of 8

SAMPLE PROBLEM-SOLVING SCENARIOS FOR KINDERGARTEN CHILDREN

Stuck Lid

Kelly and Ronald were trying to open a jar of mustard. The top of the jar would not move in any direction. How could they get the jar open?

It's Raining!

Franklin and Odessa were drawing on the sidewalk. A big drop of water hit the sidewalk; it was beginning to rain! How could Franklin and Odessa keep their pictures from getting wet?

How Do We Get Down?

Sammy and Ortega were climbing a tree when one of the limbs below them broke. How could the boys get out of the tree safely?

Can We Share?

Rosetta and Harriett wanted to look at the same book. How could the girls solve the problem of wanting to look at the book at the same time?

Dilemma

Jackson and Tomeka found a new toy car on the playground during recess. What should they do with the car?

PROBLEM-SOLVING SCENARIOS FOR YOUNG CHILDREN

Page 8 of 8

SAMPLE PROBLEM-SOLVING SCENARIOS FOR FIRST-GRADE CHILDREN

Going to the Grocery

Chris and Sara want to help Grandmother make a grocery list. What should they do first to help her?

Packing for a Picnic

What are three important things you need to pack for a picnic lunch? Why?

Going Fishing

Describe the situation:

Mario and his father were getting ready to go fishing. Here's what they put in the trunk of their car:

> *Three cans of bug spray*
> *A sack lunch with baloney sandwiches and apples*
> *An ice chest of water and soft drinks*
> *A box of curtains to take to the church rummage sale after their fishing trip*

Ask the children:

▶ Will Mario and his father need everything they packed?
Uh oh! Mario forgot to pack the sunscreen! How can he and his father keep the sun off of them while fishing?

▶ What else might they need?
(fishing poles, etc.)

The Ice Cream Truck

Trent and Danisha want to get ice cream from the ice cream truck. Each one has a dollar. They both want a triple-scoop fudge and banana cream combination, and it costs two dollars. How can the children get to eat the ice cream they want?

Source
Grace, C. (2008). *Promoting emotional resilience in young children.* Mississippi State, MS: Mississippi State University Early Childhood Institute.

CHILD SAFETY PRECAUTIONS

Page 1 of 2

Before the Planning Session

- ☐ Review the relevant material in the section "Responsibilities of the Staff" (refer to page 28) and prepare to discuss.

- ☐ Schedule one or more staff planning periods, depending on the size of your program's staff.

- ☐ Make copies of the Child Safety Checklist (see page 82) for all participating staff members.

- ☐ Select individual staff members or teams to inspect each area of the facility (make a separate list if necessary):

  Area   Employee(s)

  _____   _____

  _____   _____

  _____   _____

  _____   _____

  _____   _____

- ☐ Complete the top portion of the checklist for each individual or team and highlight all items they should check.

- ☐ Make a copy of the Staff Planning Session Roster (see page 99) (multiple pages if necessary).

- ☐ Review the next section and decide whether to complete the session in 2 hours or allot more time.

During the Planning Session

- ☐ Review the Goal and Objectives of the session:

  Goal |
  - ▶ To reduce the risk of injuries, illnesses, and stress for children in our early childhood program in the event of a disaster.

  Objectives |
  - ▶ To raise staff awareness of safety precautions
  - ▶ To inspect the entire facility using the Child Safety Checklist, noting items that need repair or updating
  - ▶ To make all possible repairs and changes

- ☐ Assign employees or teams of employees to inspect areas of the facility using the Child Safety Checklist.

Page 2 of 2

☐ Distribute the copies of the Child Safety Checklist to the designated staff members and review the procedures.

☐ Give employees time to inspect their assigned areas of the facility.

☐ Reconvene after sufficient time and ask staff members and teams to report their findings.

☐ Discuss which modifications can be made during the planning session.

☐ Complete this segment by inviting questions and discussion. Note questions that need follow-up here:

_____

_____

_____

_____

_____

☐ Give staff members and teams time to return to their inspection areas and make all possible modifications.

☐ Have all participants complete the Staff Planning Session Roster.

After the Planning Session

☐ Compile all checklists and review items that need to be completed.

☐ Schedule needed non-structural modifications, working with contractors and/or volunteers as needed.

☐ Follow up with staff on all questions and comments that you recorded.

INFECTION CONTROL

Page 1 of 3

Before the Planning Session

- [ ] Review the relevant material in the section Responsibilities of the Staff (see pages 28–30) and prepare to discuss.

- [ ] Schedule one or more staff planning periods, depending on the size of your program's staff.

- [ ] Gather containers of liquid soap, rolls of paper towels, and boxes of tissues for all classrooms and areas of the facility.

- [ ] Make copies of the handout Basic Rules of Infection Control (see page 58).

- [ ] Obtain information from the local public health agency about annual influenza vaccinations; make copies for staff and children's parents and guardians.

- [ ] Obtain information from the local public health agency about local planning for possible epidemics.

- [ ] Make a copy of the Staff Planning Session Roster (see page 99)(multiple pages if necessary).

- [ ] Review the next section and decide whether to complete the session in 2 hours or allot more time.

During the Planning Session

- [ ] Review the Goal and Objectives of the session:

  Goal |
  - To reduce the spread of infection at our early childhood program during disease outbreaks and at all times

  Objectives |
  - To know the basic rules of infection control
  - To equip all areas of the facility with supplies for infection control
  - To understand the responsibilities of early childhood professionals in disease outbreaks

- [ ] Distribute and review the handout Basic Rules of Infection Control.

- [ ] Distribute supplies for infection control to employees for placement in all classrooms and areas of the facility.

INFECTION CONTROL

Page 2 of 3

☐ Complete this segment of the planning session by inviting questions and discussion. Note questions that need follow-up here:

_____

_____

_____

_____

_____

☐ Introduce and review any information from the local public health agency about planning for epidemics.

☐ Discuss employees' responsibilities to remain home if they become ill with a contagious disease.

☐ Clearly communicate policies on sick leave and employee compensation during disease outbreaks.

☐ Have all participants complete the Staff Planning Session Roster.

After the Planning Session

☐ Follow up with staff on all questions and comments that you recorded.

☐ Send copies of information about annual influenza vaccinations home to parents and guardians.

BASIC RULES OF INFECTION CONTROL

Page 3 of 3

Post these rules in your classroom or work area.

- Stock bathrooms and all sink locations with soap and paper towels or working hand dryers.
- Stock all areas with boxes of tissues and trash cans for used tissues.
- Wash hands whenever possible between contacts with different children and after touching a child's nose or mouth, helping with toileting or diaper-changing, or providing first aid or injections.
- Wear disposable latex gloves for any possible contact with blood or other bodily fluids such as urine, feces, vomit, or nasal discharge.
- Wash hands after removing disposable gloves.
- Use soap and water to wash visibly soiled hands.
- Use an alcohol-based cleanser when soap is not available or hands are not visibly soiled. **Safety note:** Keep alcohol-based cleansers and all disinfectants out of children's reach.
- Help infants and toddlers wash their hands with soap and water before and after eating, and after sneezing or toileting.
- Teach toddlers to wash their hands for 15–20 seconds before and after eating, sneezing, or toileting.
- Remind and help children to wash their hands for 15–20 seconds before and after eating, and after sneezing or toileting, even after they have mastered the skill.
- Teach toddlers to cover their noses and mouths when sneezing or coughing and to throw away soiled tissues.
- Clean frequently used toys and materials daily, using a household disinfectant labeled for bacteria and viruses.

Sources

Centers for Disease Control and Prevention. (n.d.). *Preventing spread of the flu in child care settings: Guidance for administrators, care providers, and other staff.* Retrieved Jan. 8, 2009, from http://www.cdc.gov/flu/professionals/infectioncontrol/childcaresettings.htm

Dailey, L. (2004). *Standards and universal precautions in the child care setting.* Berkeley, CA: California Childcare Health Program. Retrieved Jan. 8, 2009, from http://www.ucsfchildcarehealth.org/pdfs/healthandsafety/standardprecen020305_adr.pdf

BASIC AND ADVANCED FIRST AID

Page 1 of 2

Before the Planning Session

☐ Review the relevant material in the section "Responsibilities of the Staff" (see pages 30–31) and prepare to discuss.

☐ Schedule one or more staff planning periods, depending on the size of your program's staff.

☐ Select employees, including yourself and your director-designate, to receive advanced first aid training during concurrent planning sessions (use a separate sheet for the list if necessary):

_____

_____

_____

_____

_____

☐ Schedule outside trainers to deliver first aid training, planning concurrent sessions for basic and advanced, and multiple sessions for advanced training, if necessary:

TOPIC	TRAINER	DATE
Basic First Aid Kits	_____	_____
Bites	_____	_____
Broken Bones	_____	_____
Burns	_____	_____
Chemical Burns	_____	_____
Chemical in Eye	_____	_____
Cuts	_____	_____
Dehydration	_____	_____
Electrical Shock	_____	_____
Eye Injuries	_____	_____
Falls	_____	_____
Head Injuries	_____	_____
Severe Bleeding	_____	_____
Shock	_____	_____

TOPIC	TRAINER	DATE
Storing Human Remains	_____	_____
Sudden Cardiac Arrest	_____	_____
Tooth Loss	_____	_____
Transporting Victims	_____	_____
Vomiting	_____	_____

☐ Make copies of the Staff Planning Session Roster (see page 99) (multiple pages if necessary) for each session.

During the Planning Session(s)

☐ Have all participants complete the Staff Planning Session Roster.

After the Planning Session(s)

☐ Follow up with staff on all questions and comments.

SHELTERING IN PLACE

Page 1 of 3

Before the Planning Session

☐ Review the relevant material in the section "Responsibilities of the Staff" (see pages 32–34) and prepare to discuss.

☐ Schedule one or more staff planning periods, depending on the size of your program's staff.

☐ If you have not already done so, complete Shelter-in-Place Diagrams (page 96) for all classrooms and areas of the facility.

☐ Review the Shelter-in-Place Procedures (see page 97) and make copies for participating staff members.

☐ Make copies of completed Shelter-in-Place Diagram(s) for all classrooms and common areas.

☐ Make copies of the Shelter-in-Place Checklist (see page 93) for individual employees or teams of employees to use in inspecting shelter-in-place location(s).

☐ Make a copy of the Staff Planning Session Roster (see page 99) (multiple pages if necessary).

☐ Review the next section and decide whether to complete the session in 2 hours or allot more time.

During the Planning Session

☐ Review the Goal and Objectives of the session:

Goal |
- ▸ To safely protect children during fires, external security threats, or other disasters that require sheltering in place

Objectives |
- ▸ To know the designated shelter-in-place location for each classroom and common area in the facility
- ▸ To review procedures for sheltering in place
- ▸ To check equipment and supplies in each designated shelter-in-place location

☐ Distribute Shelter-in-Place Diagrams for all classrooms and common areas and engage staff members in highlighting routes from their classrooms or areas to their designated shelter-in-place locations.

SHELTERING IN PLACE

Page 2 of 3

☐ Complete this segment by inviting questions and discussion. Note questions that need follow-up here:

_____

_____

_____

_____

_____

☐ Instruct staff members to post the Shelter-in-Place Diagrams in their classrooms or areas.

☐ Distribute and review copies of Shelter-in-Place Procedures.

☐ Complete this segment by inviting questions and discussion. Note questions that need follow-up here:

_____

_____

_____

_____

_____

☐ Distribute and review copies of the Shelter-in-Place Checklist.

☐ Assign individual staff members or teams to use the checklist to inspect the furnishings and equipment in shelter-in-place locations and to report missing items.

SHELTERING IN PLACE

Page 3 of 3

☐ Complete this segment of the planning session by noting missing items from shelter-in-place locations here:

_____

_____

_____

_____

_____

_____

_____

_____

_____

_____

_____

_____

_____

_____

_____

_____

_____

_____

☐ Have all participants complete the Staff Planning Session Roster.

After the Planning Session

☐ Follow up with staff on all questions and comments that you recorded.

☐ Stock or replace all missing items from shelter-in-place locations.

BUILDING EVACUATION

Page 1 of 3

Before the Planning Session

☐ Review the relevant material in the section "Responsibilities of the Staff" (see pages 35–36) and prepare to discuss.

☐ Schedule one or more staff planning periods, depending on the size of your program's staff.

☐ Make copies of the completed Essential Records Back-Up Worksheet (see pages 88–89) for all employees who handle essential records.

☐ Make copies of completed Building Evacuation Plan(s).

☐ Obtain plastic badge holders with safety pins and clips attached for teachers to use in creating Child Identity Tags.

☐ Reproduce the Child Identity Tag (page 81) on sturdy paper, trimmed to fit in the badge holders, for teachers to use in creating Child Identity Tags.

☐ Prepare evacuation kits (see list, page 82) for each group or class and program vehicle.

☐ Bring children's medical records to the planning session for teachers to use in completing Child Identity Tags.

☐ Make a copy of the Staff Planning Session Roster (see page 99) (multiple pages if necessary).

☐ Review the next section and decide whether to complete the session in 2 hours or allot more time.

During the Planning Session

☐ Review the Goals and Objective of the session:

Goals |
- To evacuate children safely from the facility during fires, earthquakes, interior security threats, or other disasters
- To maintain the security of essential child and business records from loss from fire, earthquake, or other disaster

Objectives |
- To practice building evacuations during fires, earthquakes, and interior security threats
- To review procedures for the security of essential child and business records

---

BUILDING EVACUATION

Page 2 of 3

☐ Distribute and review copies of the Essential Records Back-Up Worksheet (see page 88–89), discussing each type of record.

☐ Show the contents of an evacuation kit (see page 82) and discuss where in the facility these will be stored.

☐ Distribute materials for Child Identity Tags and engage teachers in completing tags for the children in their rooms.

☐ Complete this segment of the planning session by inviting questions and discussion. Note questions that need follow-up here:

_____

_____

_____

_____

_____

☐ Distribute and review the copies of completed Building Evacuation Plan(s), emphasizing the staff's responsibilities to:
- ▶ Assign adults to assist non-ambulatory children,
- ▶ Gather children as quickly as possible; use the buddy system,
- ▶ Gather essential prescription medications,
- ▶ Remain calm so you can calm the children,
- ▶ Carry cell phones,
- ▶ Do not use elevators,
- ▶ Once children are secure, call 911 or the local emergency management agency to request rescue:

_____
(Emergency Management Agency telephone number)

- ▶ Pin Child Identity Tags to children as soon as they are safely outside the building, and
- ▶ Notify parents as soon as children are safe.

BUILDING EVACUATION

Page 3 of 3

☐ Conduct a state-required fire drill.

OR

☐ Lead the staff outside the building(s) to designated gathering location(s), dividing the staff into teams if necessary.

☐ Complete this segment by inviting questions and discussion. Note questions that need follow-up here:

_____

_____

_____

_____

_____

☐ Instruct staff members to post the Building Evacuation Plans in their classrooms or areas.

☐ Have all participants complete the Staff Planning Session Roster.

After the Planning Session

☐ Follow up with staff on all questions and comments that you recorded.

☐ Send copies of completed Building Evacuation Plan(s) home to all parents.

☐ Store evacuation kits, including completed Child Identity Tags, in all program vehicles and near all exits.

OFF-SITE RELOCATION

Page 1 of 3

Before the Planning Session

☐ Review the relevant material in the section Responsibilities of the Staff (see pages 37–38) and prepare to discuss.

☐ Schedule one or more staff planning periods, depending on the size of your program's staff.

☐ Make copies of completed Off-Site Relocation Plan(s) (page 94) for posting at all exits and for all staff members.

☐ Prepare evacuation kits (see list on page 82) for each group or class.

☐ Make copies of the program's field trip procedures, if available.

☐ Determine what employees are covered by the facility's auto insurance as drivers.

☐ Designate employees to drive groups of children during off-site relocations (use multiple sheets if necessary):

☐ Employee(s)

_____

_____

_____

_____

_____

☐ Obtain copies of state highway maps for all program vehicles and for all designated drivers.

☐ Make a copy of the Staff Planning Session Roster (see page 99) (multiple pages if necessary).

☐ Review the next section and decide whether to complete the session in 2 hours or allot more time.

During the Planning Session

☐ Review the Goal and Objectives of the session:

Goal | ▸ To evacuate children safely from the facility during fires, earthquakes, interior security threats, or other disasters

OFF-SITE RELOCATION

Page 2 of 3

Objectives |
- To know the program's designated off-site relocation sites
- To identify designated drivers for off-site relocation
- To practice escorting children to vehicles for off-site relocation
- To review maps and directions to designated off-site relocation sites

☐ Distribute and discuss completed Off-Site Relocation Plan(s).

☐ Show the contents of an evacuation kit (see page 82) and discuss where in the facility these will be stored.

☐ Distribute and review state highway maps, pointing out relocation sites and routes from the facility.

☐ Complete this segment by inviting questions and discussion. Note questions that need follow-up here:

_____

_____

_____

_____

☐ Discuss the program's field trip procedures and compare them to procedures for off-site relocation during a disaster.

☐ Complete this segment by inviting questions and discussion. Note questions that need follow-up here:

_____

_____

_____

_____

☐ Discuss communication during an off-site relocation:

_____

_____

_____

_____

OFF-SITE RELOCATION

Page 3 of 3

☐ Drivers should communicate with the director or director-designate while traveling to relocation sites and upon arrival.

☐ The director or director-designate will coordinate communication with parents and guardians.

☐ Have all participants complete the Staff Planning Session Roster.

After the Planning Session

☐ Follow up with staff on all questions and comments that you recorded.

☐ Send copies of completed Off-Site Relocation Plan(s) home to all parents and guardians.

☐ Store evacuation kits (see page 82), including highway maps and Off-Site Relocation Plans, in all program vehicles and near all exits.

HELPING CHILDREN COPE AFTER DISASTERS

Page 1 of 5

Before the Planning Session

☐ Obtain and review the recommended readings below (Schedule enough time for this step to allow for interlibrary loans):

☐ Alat, K. (2002). Traumatic events and children: How early childhood educators can help. *Childhood Education* 79(1): 2–8.

☐ Demaree, M.A. (1995). Creating safe environments for children with post-traumatic stress disorder. *Dimensions of Early Childhood* 23(3): 31–33, 40.

☐ Devall, E.L., & Cahill, B.J. (1995). Addressing children's life changes in the early childhood curriculum. *Early Childhood Education Journal* 23(2): 57–62.

☐ Szente, J., Hoot, J., & Taylor, D. (2006). Responding to the special needs of refugee children: Practical ideas for teachers. *Early Childhood Education Journal,* 34(1), 15–20.

☐ Review the relevant material in the section Responsibilities of the Staff (see pages 39–43) and prepare to discuss.

☐ Schedule one or more staff planning periods, depending on the size of your program's staff.

☐ Review the Library List in *After the Crisis: Using Storybooks to Help Children Cope* and visit a public library to obtain copies of selected children's books. (Schedule enough time for this step to allow for interlibrary loans.)

☐ Prepare to discuss the recommended readings during the planning session.

☐ Assign individual staff members to summarize readings during the planning session:

Staff Member	Reading
_____	Alat, "Traumatic Events and Children"
_____	Demaree, "Creating Safe Environments"
_____	Devall & Cahill, "Addressing Children's Life Changes"
_____	Szente, Hoot & Taylor, "Special Needs of Refugee Children"

HELPING CHILDREN COPE AFTER DISASTERS

Page 2 of 5

☐ Make copies of the referral form, provided by your cooperating mental health agency, for evaluation of possible stress disorders or other social-emotional problems.

☐ Review, or assign a teacher or pair of teachers to review, *After the Crisis: Using Storybooks to Help Children Cope* before the planning session.

☐ Review library copies and select children's books for demonstration in the workshop; assign teacher(s) to demonstrate the literature-based activities:

Teacher: _____

Title: _____

Teacher: _____

Title: _____

Teacher: _____

Title: _____

☐ Make a copy of the Staff Planning Session Roster on page 99 (multiple pages if necessary).

☐ Review the next section and decide whether to complete the session in 2 hours or allot more time.

During the Planning Session

☐ Review the Goal and Objectives of the session:

Goal | ▸ To help children cope after experiencing disasters

Objectives | ▸ To be able to define Traumatic Stress Disorder and discuss how it may affect young children

▸ To be able to list and discuss the five responsibilities of early childhood teachers for helping young children cope with traumatic experiences

▸ To practice literature-based activities for helping children cope with the aftermath of disasters

HELPING CHILDREN COPE AFTER DISASTERS

Page 3 of 5

☐ Introduce the concept of Traumatic Stress Disorder, emphasizing these key points:

- ‣ Very young children can suffer from Traumatic Stress Disorder.
- ‣ Children with possible stress disorder must receive assessment, diagnosis, and treatment.

☐ Referring to the material in Staff Responsibilities, (see pages 39–43) introduce and discuss the responsibilities of early childhood teachers to:

- ‣ Manage their own stress,
- ‣ Provide a safe environment for young children,
- ‣ Provide outlets for children's expression,
- ‣ Observe and record signs of possible stress disorders, and
- ‣ Participate in referrals to mental health professionals.

☐ Ask designated staff members to summarize the assigned readings:

☐ _____ Alat, "Traumatic Events and Children"

☐ _____ Demaree, "Creating Safe Environments"

☐ _____ Devall & Cahill, "Addressing Children's Life Changes"

☐ _____ Szente, Hoot & Taylor, "Special Needs of Refugee Children"

☐ Discuss these ideas for providing a safe environment for children who have experienced disasters:

- ‣ Give physical comfort
- ‣ Listen and respond
- ‣ Create a predictable routine
- ‣ Support transitions
- ‣ Provide quiet areas
- ‣ Provide times for outdoor play
- ‣ Avoid time-outs

☐ Complete this segment by inviting questions and discussion. Note questions that need follow-up here:

_____

_____

_____

_____

HELPING CHILDREN COPE AFTER DISASTERS

Page 4 of 5

☐ Introduce the concept of anecdotal record-keeping (see page 43) and discuss these tips:
  ▸ Keep a pencil and pad with you at all times.
  ▸ Make quick notes to yourself when you notice new or unusual behaviors that might indicate a stress disorder.
  ▸ Date your notes.
  ▸ Within the day, write clear, concise anecdotal records based upon your quick notes.
  ▸ Be careful to report the facts without trying to interpret or explain them.
  ▸ Place each original record in the child's folder or portfolio and give a copy to your supervisor.

☐ Distribute and review the referral form, provided by your cooperating mental health agency, for evaluation of possible stress disorders or other social-emotional problems.

☐ Complete this segment by inviting questions and discussion. Note questions that need follow-up here:

_____

_____

_____

_____

_____

☐ Invite teachers to discuss classroom outlets for children's expression.

☐ Discuss these tips for using books to support children's creative expressions:
  ▸ Introduce each book by reading the title, author's name, and illustrator's name, pointing to each on the cover or initial pages.
  ▸ Encourage the children to comment on the book as you read it aloud. Pause whenever the children want to discuss the story or illustrations.
  ▸ If the book does not hold the children's interest, shorten the reading by discussing the events in the story without reading the book line-by-line. This is a good approach with books that have a useful topic but are too advanced for the children.
  ▸ After you introduce the book in this way, proceed with the discussion starters we suggest as well as any other questions you want to add. Set up and explain materials and optional activities for the art and writing centers in the classroom.

HELPING CHILDREN COPE AFTER DISASTERS

Page 5 of 5

☐ Call upon designated teacher(s) to demonstrate selected literature-based activities in the curriculum.

☐ Discuss where in your center teachers will keep books for literature-based activities so they can be rotated through classrooms; assign one teacher to coordinate the rotation of books.

☐ Complete this segment by inviting questions and discussion. Note questions that need follow-up here:

_____

_____

_____

_____

_____

☐ Have all participants complete the Staff Planning Session Roster.

After the Planning Session

☐ Follow up with staff on all questions and comments that you recorded.

DISASTER READINESS WORKSHEETS

4

Note: Make copies of these worksheets and preserve the original blank worksheets to use in the following years.

Page 1 of 3

Complete this plan for each calendar year (January–December) or fiscal year (July–June). Please print.

Early Childhood Program Name   Calendar or Fiscal Year

Director   State License or Registration Number (if applicable)

Priority 1. Identify Disaster Readiness Contacts   Target Date: _____

Enter names of agencies, contact persons, telephone numbers, and e-mail addresses.

Emergency Management Agency

Contact   Telephone   E-Mail

Public Health Agency

Contact   Telephone   E-Mail

Child Care Licensing Agency

Contact   Telephone   E-Mail

Child Care Subsidy Agency

Contact   Telephone   E-Mail

Child Nutrition Program

Contact   Telephone   E-Mail

CCR&R

Contact   Telephone   E-Mail

Priority 2. Review Regulatory Standards   **Target Date:** _____

For each set of standards or eligibility criteria that affects your program, enter specific disaster readiness requirements.

Child Care Licensing _____

_____

Child Care Subsidy Program _____

_____

Child Nutrition Program _____

_____

Quality Rating and Improvement System _____

_____

Accrediting Agency _____

_____

Priority 3. Basic Readiness Activities   **Target Date:** _____

Check each activity as you complete it for the current year.

☐ Selection of director-designate (name): _____

☐ Inventories current for business office and all classrooms

☐ Emergency Management Liaison Form (see page 87) delivered to local EMA

☐ Memorandum of understanding with a mental health agency

☐ Memorandum of understanding with a developmental services agency

☐ Facility design and architectural drawings filed with this plan

Page 3 of 3

Priority 4. Advanced Readiness Activities

Check each activity as you complete it for the current year.   **Target Dates**

☐ Building Evacuation Plan   _____

☐ Child Identity Tags   _____

☐ Disaster Insurance Worksheet   _____

☐ Disaster Fund Worksheet   _____

☐ Essential Records Back-Up Worksheet   _____

☐ Child Safety Checklist(s)   _____

☐ Shelter-in-Place Diagram (for each shelter-in-place location)   _____

☐ Shelter-in-Place Checklist (for each shelter-in-place location)   _____

☐ Off-Site Relocation Plan (for each relocation site)   _____

☐ Facility Modifications Needs Assessment   _____

☐ Copies of completed worksheets are filed with this completed plan:

     ☐ On-site

     ☐ Off-site (enter location): _____

     ☐ Off-site (enter location): _____

Priority 5. Schedule Staff Planning Sessions   Target Date: _____

Decide on 2-hour or longer sessions for each topic. Enter schedule details for all sessions and check each session as it is completed.

Topic	Date	Time	Staff Facilitator	Speaker
☐ Resilience	_____	_____	_____	_____
☐ Child Safety	_____	_____	_____	_____
☐ Infection Control	_____	_____	_____	_____
☐ First Aid	_____	_____	_____	_____
☐ Shelter in Place	_____	_____	_____	_____
☐ Building Evacuation	_____	_____	_____	_____
☐ Off-Site Relocation	_____	_____	_____	_____
☐ Helping Children Cope	_____	_____	_____	_____

☐ Staff Planning Participation Log completed

AGENCY CONTACT SHEET

_____
Early Childhood Program Name

_____
State License or Registration Number (if applicable)

During and after a disaster, record notes of each contact with a regulatory or funding agency. Attach hard copies of e-mail messages, if available.

_____
Date

_____
Agency

_____
Contact

Notes:
_____

_____

_____
Date

_____
Agency

_____
Contact

Notes:
_____

_____

_____
Date

_____
Agency

_____
Contact

Notes:
_____

_____

Early Childhood Program Name:

State License or Registration Number (if applicable)

Date:

Room or Area

In a building evacuation, we will hold children at the evacuation site indicated below.

Evacuation Procedure

▶ Assign an evacuation leader

▶ Assign adults to assist non-ambulatory children

▶ Gather children as quickly as possible; use the buddy system

▶ Gather evacuation kits (see page 82) and essential prescription medications

▶ Remain calm so you can calm the children

▶ Carry cell phones

▶ Do not use elevators

▶ Escort children to evacuation locations

▶ Once children are secure, call 911 or the local emergency management agency to request rescue:

(Emergency Management Agency telephone number)

▶ Pin Child Identity Tags to children as soon as they are safely outside the building

If necessary, retype the information for the Child Identity Tags to fit inside plastic badge holders with clips and safety pins attached.

First Name   Last Name

School/Child Care Facility

School/Child Care Facility Emergency Telephone

Parent/Guardian Name

Home Address

Home Telephone   Cell Phone

Medical Conditions

Allergies

Medications and Dosage

First Name   Last Name

School/Child Care Facility

School/Child Care Facility Emergency Telephone

Parent/Guardian Name

Home Address

Home Telephone   Cell Phone

Medical Conditions

Allergies

Medications and Dosage

Date
_____

Facility Name
_____

State License or Registration Number (if applicable)
_____

Room or Area

Carefully inspect the room(s) or area(s) of the child care facility for all of the items on this checklist, checking items that need changes or repairs. After completing your inspection, return this checklist to the facility's administrator.

CHILD SAFETY PRECAUTIONS

- [ ] NOAA weather radio with tone alert feature and battery back-up is kept in central location and continually on
- [ ] Computers with business and child records have UL-listed surge protectors and battery back-up systems
- [ ] Chemicals (bleach, paint thinner, cleaners, etc.) are stored securely in locked cabinets
- [ ] All drawers and cabinets have baby-proof latches so they cannot swing or roll open accidentally
- [ ] Blocks and heavy objects are stored on lowest shelves
- [ ] Cribs are placed away from the tops of stairs and other locations where they could roll or heavy objects could fall on them
- [ ] Tall cribs are anchored to prevent tipping
- [ ] Heavy and sharp items are stored on shelves with ledges
- [ ] TV sets, computers, aquariums, potted plants and other heavy items are secured or restrained so they cannot slide
- [ ] Battery-powered emergency lights are stored in all rooms
- [ ] Batteries are working in all emergency lights
- [ ] Pipe or crescent wrench stored beside each water and gas source
- [ ] Shelter-in-Place Procedures are posted
- [ ] Building Evacuation Plan(s) are posted
- [ ] Evacuation kits, stored in each program vehicle and near each exit, are fully furnished:
  - [ ] First aid supplies
  - [ ] Goggles for all children and adults
  - [ ] Disposable breathing masks for all children and adults
  - [ ] Child Identity Tags
  - [ ] Child and employee rosters
  - [ ] Current Off-Site Relocation Plan(s)
  - [ ] Current state highway map

DISASTER FUND WORKSHEET

Page 1 of 2

Early Childhood Program Name

State License or Registration Number (if applicable)

Fiscal or Calendar Year

1. Calculate Annual Operating Expenses

Payroll	$ _____
Insurance Premiums	_____
Fire	_____
Flood	_____
Wind	_____
Other	_____
Rent or Mortgage Payments	_____
Utility Payments	_____
Electricity	_____
Gas	_____
Water	_____
Sewer	_____
Internet	_____
Transportation Costs	_____
Vehicle Payments/Insurance	_____
Gasoline	_____
Purchases	_____
Classroom Materials	_____
Food	_____
Office Supplies	_____
Other	_____
Total	$ _____

2. Calculate One-Month Disaster Fund

Divide Annual Operating Expenses by 12: $ _____

3. Calculate Monthly Disaster Fund Savings

Divide One-Month Disaster Fund by 12: $ _____

4. Budget for Monthly Disaster Fund Savings

Reduce Expenditures:	Increase Revenues:
Type: _____	Type: _____
Amount: $ _____	Amount: $ _____
Type: _____	Type: _____
Amount: $ _____	Amount: $ _____
Type: _____	Type: _____
Amount: $ _____	Amount: $ _____
Subtotal: $ _____	Subtotal: $ _____

5. Add the sub-totals in Step 4 and deposit to Disaster Fund account.

DISASTER INSURANCE WORKSHEET

Page 1 of 2

Early Childhood Program Name

State License or Registration Number (if applicable)

Fiscal or Calendar Year

Our program has the following kinds of insurance against disasters.

☐ Commercial Property Insurance

This policy covers repairs of damages from:

☐ Fire damage

☐ Wind damage

☐ Explosions

☐ Other:_____

Provider

Policy Number

Amount

Local Agent

Telephone

Alternate Telephone

Mailing Address

Policy Renewal Date

Structural Modifications to Reduce Premiums

☐ Homeowner Insurance

This policy covers repairs of damages from:

☐ Fire damage

☐ Wind damage

☐ Explosions

☐ Other:_____

Provider

Policy Number

Amount

Page 2 of 2

Local Agent

Telephone

Alternate Telephone

Mailing Address

Policy Renewal Date

Structural Modifications to Reduce Premiums

☐ Earthquake Insurance

Provider

Policy Number

Amount

Local Agent

Telephone

Alternate Telephone

Mailing Address

Policy Renewal Date

Structural Modifications to Reduce Premiums

☐ Flood Insurance

Provider

Policy Number

Amount

Local Agent

Telephone

Alternate Telephone

Mailing Address

Policy Renewal Date

Structural Modifications to Reduce Premiums

EMERGENCY MANAGEMENT LIAISON FORM

_____

Early Childhood Program Name

_____

State License or Registration Number (if applicable)

_____

Fiscal or Calendar Year

The following information is provided to (insert name of emergency management agency) _____ **to inform the agency of the location and likely enrollment of an early childhood program for purposes of search and rescue operations and to request recommendations by the EMA of off-site relocation routes and destinations for this early childhood program.**

_____

Early Childhood Program Director   Date

By this signature, a representative of (insert name of emergency management agency) _____ **acknowledges receipt of this information.**

_____

EMA Representative   Date

_____

Director's First Name   Director's Last Name

_____

Telephone   Back-Up Telephone

_____

Street Address

_____

City/State/Zip

_____

Emergency Contact Name

_____

Emergency Contact Telephone

_____

Emergency Contact Back-Up Telephone

_____

Age Range of Children

_____

Maximum Enrollment   Average Enrollment

_____

Summer Enrollment   School Break Enrollment

_____

Number of Children with Special Needs (wheelchair, speech, etc.):

Page 1 of 2

Early Childhood Program Name

State License or Registration Number (if applicable)

Fiscal or Calendar Year

Type of Record	Format		Location	Frequency of Backup		
	Paper	Electronic		Day	Week	Month
Child Roster*	☐	☐				
Employee Roster*	☐	☐				
Child Progress						
Developmental Checklists	☐	☐		☐	☐	☐
Anecdotal Records	☐	☐		☐	☐	☐
Work Samples	☐	☐		☐	☐	☐
Child Enrollment						
ID/Medical Tag	☐	☐		☐	☐	☐
Entry Form	☐	☐		☐	☐	☐
Exit Form	☐	☐		☐	☐	☐
Referrals	☐	☐		☐	☐	☐
Child Care Assistance	☐	☐		☐	☐	☐
Child Nutrition	☐	☐		☐	☐	☐
Others:	☐	☐		☐	☐	☐
	☐	☐		☐	☐	☐
	☐	☐		☐	☐	☐
Personnel						
Employment Application	☐	☐		☐	☐	☐
Others:	☐	☐		☐	☐	☐
	☐	☐		☐	☐	☐
	☐	☐		☐	☐	☐

Type of Record	Format		Location	Frequency of Backup		
	Paper	Electronic		Day	Week	Month
Business						
Incorporation papers	☐	☐		☐	☐	☐
Facility/lease or deed	☐	☐		☐	☐	☐
Insurance records	☐	☐		☐	☐	☐
Contracts with grantors:						
	☐	☐		☐	☐	☐
	☐	☐		☐	☐	☐
	☐	☐		☐	☐	☐
Contracts with vendors:						
	☐	☐		☐	☐	☐
	☐	☐		☐	☐	☐
	☐	☐		☐	☐	☐
Business						
Federal Tax Exemption	☐	☐		☐	☐	☐
State Tax Exemption	☐	☐		☐	☐	☐
Federal Tax Returns	☐	☐		☐	☐	☐
State Tax Returns	☐	☐		☐	☐	☐
Others:	☐	☐		☐	☐	☐
	☐	☐		☐	☐	☐
	☐	☐		☐	☐	☐

*Including local and distant emergency contact numbers

Date

Facility Name

State License or Registration Number (if applicable)

Contractor or EMA Representative

Business or Agency

Telephone

Carefully inspect all room(s) or area(s) of the child care facility for all of the items in this checklist, checking items that need modification.

DONE	DEADLINE	RESPONSIBLE PARTY	ITEM
☐			Appliances, cabinets, and shelves are attached to the wall with brackets or anchored together
☐			Pictures and other wall hangings are attached with wire and closed screw-eyes
☐			Heavy furnishings and equipment are latched or tethered to walls when not in use
☐			Fire extinguishers are secured to walls with brackets
☐			Suspended ceilings are secured to structural framing
☐			Suspended light fixtures are attached to structural framing with safety cables
☐			Fluorescent lights have transparent sleeves to prevent broken glass pieces from scattering
☐			Battery-powered emergency lights are secured to walls with brackets
☐			Blackboards and projection screens are securely mounted to the wall or ceiling
☐			Top and bottom of water heater are secured to wall studs (not just gypsum board)
☐			Gas appliances (including water heaters) have flexible connectors, not rigid connectors
☐			Large sheet-metal heating-ventilating-air conditioning ducts have diagonal bracing above or enough vertical support straps to keep any section from falling

DONE	DEADLINE	RESPONSIBLE PARTY	ITEM
☐			Lightweight panels, not shelving units or other tall furnishings, are used to divide rooms
☐			Heavy or tall room dividers are braced by interconnecting them in L-shapes or zigzags
☐			Any partitions that extend to a suspended ceiling are supported by the structure above, especially if they are used to anchor heavy items in the room
☐			No trees in poor health are leaning near the building
☐			Street number of the facility is clearly visible from roadway

Earthquake and Hurricane Risk Areas

DONE	DEADLINE	RESPONSIBLE PARTY	ITEM
☐			Building frame needs steel bracing
☐			Building frame needs shear walls
☐			Columns are strengthened
☐			Unreinforced chimney is braced
☐			Unreinforced masonry and concrete walls are braced
☐			Foundation secured by anchor bolts and/or hold-down clamps
☐			For any new construction, voluntary and mandatory earthquake and hurricane safety codes are followed
☐			Windows and doors are impact-resistant, or plywood or metal storm shutters are ready for large windows and doors

Flood Risk Areas

DONE	DEADLINE	RESPONSIBLE PARTY	ITEM
☐			Air conditioning units, water heaters, and electrical panels are moved to the top floor
☐			Unnecessary windows, doors, or other openings are filled with water-resistant concrete blocks or bricks
☐			All drains and toilets have backflow valves to prevent floodwater from entering the building
☐			Each building has a portable pump with a back-up power source for removing floodwater

DONE	DEADLINE	RESPONSIBLE PARTY	ITEM
☐			Exterior walls are sealed to prevent or reduce water seepage
☐			Susceptible areas have watertight walls
☐			For any new construction, voluntary and mandatory flood safety codes are followed

Wildfire Risk Areas

DONE	DEADLINE	RESPONSIBLE PARTY	ITEM
☐			Trees on the property are pruned six to ten feet above the ground
☐			There is no mid-height shrubbery or vegetation that could enable fire to jump from grass to trees
☐			Trees are at least 10 feet apart
☐			All vegetation and trees on the property are native and fire-resistant
☐			Property has a well-maintained irrigation system
☐			Leaf clutter is regularly removed from roofs, gutters, and grounds
☐			Lawn is regularly mowed
☐			Firewood is stored away from the structure
☐			The building is surrounded by 30-foot zones, such as paved or gravel areas or lawns, to slow spreading fires
☐			Areas beneath decks are enclosed with noncombustible material to prevent accumulation of leaves and debris
☐			Dual- or triple-pane thermal glass in large windows and doors
☐			For any new construction, voluntary and mandatory wildfire safety codes are followed

MANDATORY CLOSING CHECKLIST

Facility Name
_____

State License or Registration Number (if applicable)
_____

Fiscal or Calendar Year
_____

For each item, designate the staff member responsible for transport and off-site storage location. Use additional sheets if necessary.

Administrative Records and Equipment

ITEM	STAFF RESPONSIBLE	OFF-SITE STORAGE LOCATION
Essential Records	_____	_____
Office Computer	_____	_____
Office Printer	_____	_____

Classroom Contents (identify classroom by age group or room number)

_____	_____	_____
_____	_____	_____
_____	_____	_____
_____	_____	_____
_____	_____	_____
_____	_____	_____
_____	_____	_____
_____	_____	_____
_____	_____	_____
_____	_____	_____

☐ Utilities shut off:
　☐ Water
　☐ Electricity
　☐ Gas
☐ Windows and doors locked and secured

Facility Name

State License or Registration Number (if applicable)

Date

Relocation Site

Name   Telephone

Address, City, State

In an off-site evacuation, we will transport children to the location indicated below.

Evacuation Procedure

▶ Assign adults to assist non-ambulatory children

▶ Gather children as quickly as possible; use the buddy system

▶ Gather evacuation kits (see page 82) and essential prescription medications

▶ Remain calm so you can calm the children

▶ Carry cell phones

▶ Carry battery-powered NOAA weather radio(s) to monitor reports of safe travel routes

▶ Do not use elevators

▶ Escort children to vehicles

▶ Once children are secure, call 911 or the local emergency management agency to request rescue:

_____

(Emergency Management Agency telephone number)

▶ Pin Child Identity Tags to children as soon as they are safely in vehicles

▶ Notify parents as soon as children are safe

SHELTER-IN-PLACE CHECKLIST

Date

Facility Name

State License or Registration Number (if applicable)

Room or Area

The shelter-in-place location has the following items:

- ☐ Shelter-in-Place Procedures are posted
- ☐ Portable generator
- ☐ Fire extinguisher
- ☐ Non-perishable foods for 72 hours
- ☐ Bottled water for 72 hours
- ☐ Non-electric can opener
- ☐ Paper plates and plastic drinking cups and utensils
- ☐ Blankets
- ☐ Complete set of clothing and footwear for each child and adult
- ☐ Washcloths (2–5 for each child and adult)
- ☐ Diapering supplies for 72 hours
- ☐ Sturdy plastic garbage bags with ties (for toileting)
- ☐ Battery-powered lights
- ☐ Battery-powered radios
- ☐ Extra batteries for lights and radios
- ☐ Extra batteries for cell phones
- ☐ Liquid soap
- ☐ First aid kits
- ☐ Emergency contact information for children
- ☐ Tools for rescue:
    - ☐ Shovels
    - ☐ Crowbars
- ☐ Materials for sealing a shelter against hazardous materials:
    - ☐ Duct tape (enough rolls for all sides of all windows, doors, and air vents)
    - ☐ Plastic sheeting (pre-cut sections to cover each window, door, and air vent)
- ☐ Books and play materials for children

_____

Facility Name

_____

State License or Registration Number (if applicable)

_____

Fiscal or Calendar Year

_____

Room Name or Number

_____

Assigned Shelter-in-Place Location

In a shelter-in-place situation, we will shelter children in the location indicated below.

Evacuation Procedure

▶ Assign an evacuation leader

▶ Assign adults to assist non-ambulatory children

▶ Gather children as quickly as possible; use the buddy system

▶ Gather evacuation kits (see page 82) and essential prescription medications

▶ Remain calm so you can calm the children

▶ Carry cell phones

▶ Do not use elevators

▶ Escort children to shelter-in-place locations

▶ Once children are secure, call 911 or the local emergency management agency to request rescue:

_____

(Emergency Management Agency telephone number)

▶ Pin Child Identity Tags to children as soon as they are safely outside the building

The lead staff member should call 911 or the local emergency management agency to request assistance or rescue:

_____
Emergency Management Agency   Telephone

- Wait for the lead staff member to provide a message to give parents and guardians by cell phone if possible
- Keep children away from doors, windows, and exterior walls
- Monitor a NOAA weather radio for warnings
- Help children take cover under sturdy furniture or braced against inside walls (if falling debris is a risk)
- Show children how to crouch down and protect their heads and necks with their arms (if falling debris is a risk)
- Shut off utilities if building damage is possible
- To seal the shelter:
  - Close and lock doors and windows
  - Close air vents and fireplace dampers
  - Switch air intakes to closed position
  - Seal doors, windows, vents, and areas around fans, air conditioners, and forced air heating units with plastic sheeting and duct tape
  - Use dampened washcloths or breathing masks to cover mouths and noses
  - Remain in the sealed area until rescuers arrive

Source

Federal Emergency Management Agency. (2006). *Emergency management guide for business and industry.* Washington, DC: Author.

Facility Name

State License or Registration Number (if applicable)

Fiscal or Calendar Year

Use multiple pages as necessary or recreate the chart in a spreadsheet program. Create a row for each employee. Enter the date when each employee attends each planning session. Check each employee who has attended all annual planning sessions.

EMPLOYEE	DATE OF EACH SESSION							
	Resilience	Safety Precautions	Infection Control	First Aid	Shelter in Place	Bldg. Evac.	Off-Site Relocation	Help Children Cope

Facility Name

State License or Registration Number (if applicable)

Staff Planning Topic

Date   Location

NAME (PLEASE PRINT)	SIGNATURE

REFERENCES

Alat, K. (2002). Traumatic events and children: How early childhood educators can help. *Childhood Education*, 79(1), 2–8.

Bailey, B. (2004). *Conscious discipline live!* Oviedo, FL: Loving Guidance.

Centers for Disease Control and Prevention. (n.d.). *Preventing spread of the flu in child care settings: Guidance for administrators, care providers, and other staff.* Retrieved Jan. 8, 2009, from http://www.cdc.gov/flu/professionals/infectioncontrol/childcaresettings.htm

Centers for Disease Control and Prevention. (2006). *Child care and preschool pandemic influenza planning checklist.* Retrieved Jan. 13, 2009, from http://www.pandemicflu.gov/plan/pdf/child_care.pdf

Dailey, L. (2004). *Standards and universal precautions in the child care setting.* Berkeley, CA: California Childcare Health Program. Retrieved Jan. 8, 2009, from http://www.ucsfchildcarehealth.org/pdfs/healthandsafety/standardprecen020305_adr.pdf

Demaree, M.A. (1995). Creating safe environments for children with post-traumatic stress disorder. *Dimensions of Early Childhood,* 23(13), 31–33, 40.

Devall, E.L., & Cahill, B.J. (1995). Addressing children's life changes in the early childhood curriculum. *Early Childhood Education Journal,* 23(2), 57–62.

Drell, M.J., Siegel, C.H., & Gaensbauer, T.J. (1993). Post-Traumatic Stress Disorder. In C.H. Zeanah (Ed.), *Handbook of infant mental health* (pp. 291–304). New York: Guilford Press.

Federal Emergency Management Agency. 2006. *Emergency management guide for business and industry.* Washington, DC: Author.

Gaensbauer, T.J. (2004). Traumatized young children: Assessment and treatment processes. In J. Osofsky (Ed.), *Young children and trauma: Intervention and treatment* (pp. 194–216). New York: Guilford Press.

Ginsburg, K.R. (2007). The importance of play in promoting healthy child development and maintaining strong parent-child bonds. *Pediatrics, 119,* 183–191.

Grace, C. (2008). *Promoting emotional resilience in young children.* Mississippi State, MS: Mississippi State University Early Childhood Institute.

Greenspan, S.I., & Wieder, S. (2006). *Infant and early childhood mental health: A comprehensive, developmental approach to assessment and intervention.* Washington, DC: American Psychiatric Publishing, Inc.

Gross, S. (2007). *Project Joy preschool playmaker basic training manual.* Brookline, MA: Project Joy.

Institute for Business and Home Safety. (1999). *Nonstructural mitigation for child care centers.* Tampa, FL: Author.

Insurance Information Institute. (2008). *Catastrophes: Insurance issues.* New York: Author. Retrieved Jan. 8, 2009, from http://www.iii.org

Kindler, A.M. (1996). Myths, habits, research, and policy: The four pillars of early childhood art education. Arts Education Policy Review, 97(4), 24–30.

Lieberman, A.F., & Van Horn, P. (2004). Assessment and treatment of young children exposed to traumatic events. In J. Osofsky (Ed.), *Young children and trauma: Intervention and treatment* (pp. 111–138). New York: Guilford Press.

Mayo Clinic. (2008). First aid guide. Retrieved Dec. 15, 2008, from
http://www.mayoclinic.com/health/firstaidindex/firstaidindex

McGinn, L.K., & Spindel, C.B. (2007). Disaster trauma. In F.M. Dattilio & A. Freeman (Eds.), Cognitive-behavioral strategies in crisis intervention (pp. 399–427). New York: Guilford Press.

Mississippi State University Early Childhood Institute. (2007). The Early Childhood Disaster Risk Index: Vulnerability and emergency preparedness needs of the early childhood sector in eleven states at high risk of hurricanes, earthquakes, or both. (Mississippi State University Early Childhood Report No. 6). Mississippi State, MS: Author.

National Association of Child Care Resource and Referral Agencies. (2006). Disaster preparation: A training program for child care centers. Washington, DC: Author.

National Association for the Education of Young Children. (n.d.). NAEYC position statement on violence in the lives of children. Washington, DC: Author. Retrieved Jan. 8, 2009, from http://www.naeyc.org/files/naeyc/file/positions/PSVIOL98.PDF

National Child Traumatic Stress Network. (2008a). Child trauma toolkit for educators. Los Angeles, CA: National Center for Child Traumatic Stress. (Accessed Dec. 10, 2008, at http://www.nctsnet.org/nctsn_assets/pdfs/preschool_children.pdf.)

National Child Traumatic Stress Network. (2008b). Psychological first aid: Field operations guide (2nd ed.). Los Angeles, CA: Author.

Oregon Natural Hazards Workgroup. (2003). Pre-disaster mitigation program: Household natural hazards preparedness survey and focus group report. Eugene, OR: Author. Retrieved Dec. 29, 2008, from http://www.oregonshowcase.org/downloads/pdf/resources/NE_Survey_Report%2006-30.pdf

Osofsky, J. (2004). Perspectives on working with traumatized young children: How to deal with the feelings emerging from trauma work. In J. Osofsky (Ed.), Young children and trauma: Intervention and treatment (pp. 326–338). New York: Guilford Press.

Scheeringa, M.S. (2008). Developmental considerations for diagnosing PTSD and acute stress disorder in preschool and school-age children. American Journal of Psychiatry 165:10, 1237–1239.

Shores, E.F., & Grace, C. (1998). The portfolio book: A step-by-step guide for teachers. Beltsville, MD: Gryphon House.

Shores, E.F., Grace, C., Barbaro, E., Flenner, M., & Barbaro, M.C. (2009). Reducing risks for young children: Indicators research can guide disaster preparedness of the early childhood sector. Child Indicators Research.

Shores, E.F., Heath, J., Barbaro, E., Barbaro, M.C., & Grace, C. (2008). Putting young children on disaster maps: The challenges of data integration. Journal of Emergency Management, 5(4), 47–56.

Somasundaram, D.J., & van de Put, W.A. (2006). Management of trauma in special populations after a disaster [Abstract]. The Journal of Clinical Psychiatry, 67 Suppl 2, 64–73.

Szente, J., Hoot, J., & Taylor, D. (2006). Responding to the special needs of refugee children: Practical ideas for teachers. Early Childhood Education Journal, 34(1), 15–20.

U.S. Department of Health and Human Services. (2007). Community strategy for pandemic influenza mitigation. Washington, DC: Author. Retrieved Dec. 18, 2008, from http://www.pandemicflu.gov/plan/community/commitigation.html#app5

INDEX